# MEN'S EDITION

# ANDREW LLOYD WEBBER™
## FOR SINGERS

ISBN 978-1-4234-3674-4

HAL•LEONARD®
CORPORATION

7777 W. BLUEMOUND RD. P.O. BOX 13819 MILWAUKEE, WI 53213

Visit Hal Leonard Online at
**www.halleonard.com**

## CONTENTS BY SONG

*Not from a show

# CONTENTS BY SHOW

# THE AD-DRESSING OF CATS

## from *Cats*

Music by ANDREW LLOYD WEBBER
Text by T.S. ELIOT

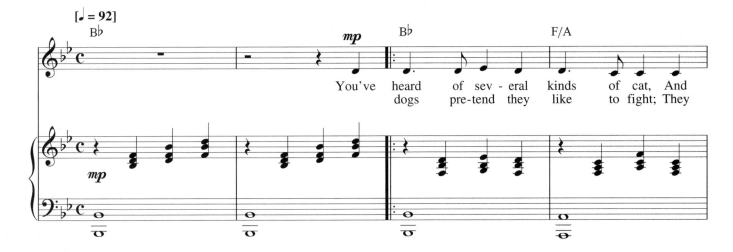

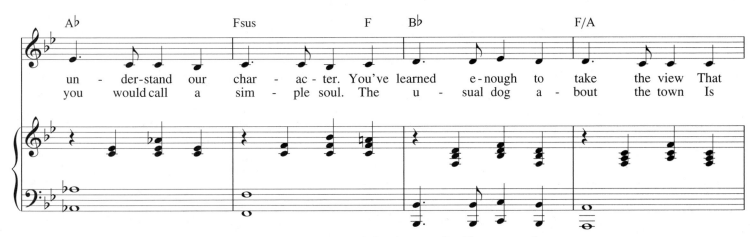

*In the show, this number is performed by Old Deuteronomy and the chorus, edited here as a solo.*

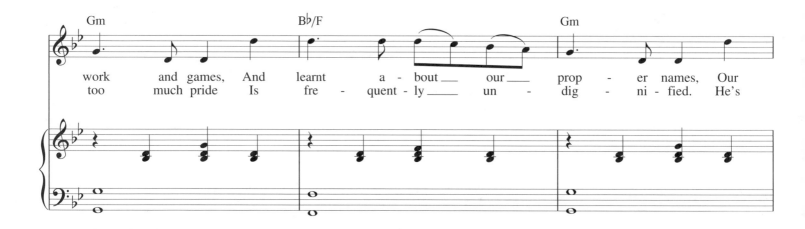

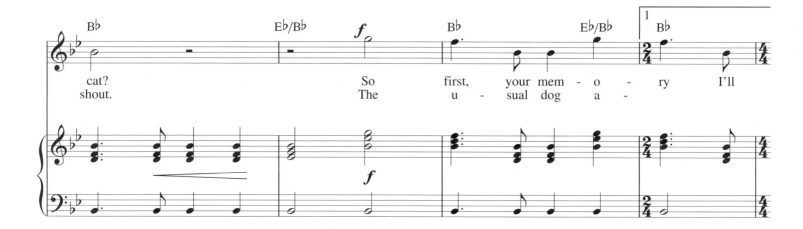

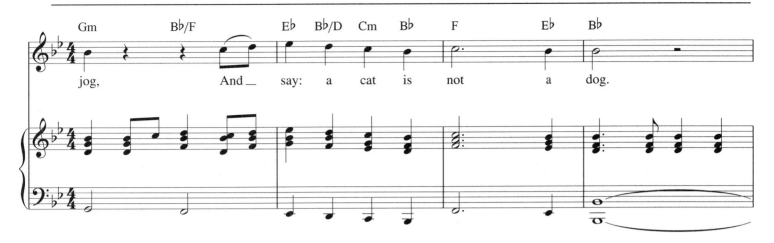

jog, And _ say: a cat is not a dog.

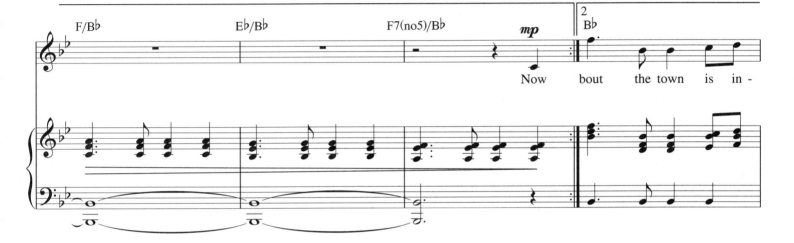

Now bout the town is in -

clined to play the clown. A - gain I must re - mind you

that A _ dog's a dog, a cat's a cat.

With cats, some say, one rule is

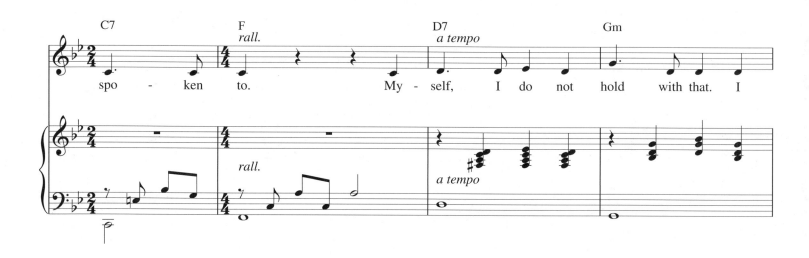

true: Don't speak till you are

spo - ken to. My - self, I do not hold with that. I

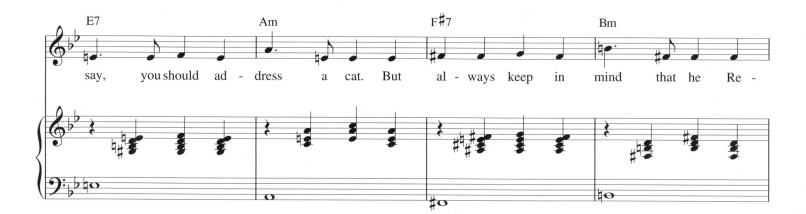

say, you should ad - dress a cat. But al - ways keep in mind that he Re -

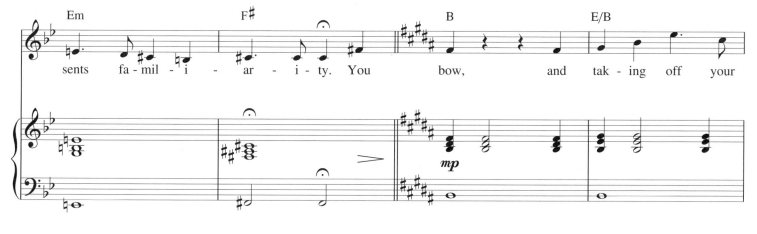

sents fa - mil - i - ar - i - ty. You bow, and tak - ing off your

hat, ad - dress him in this form: O

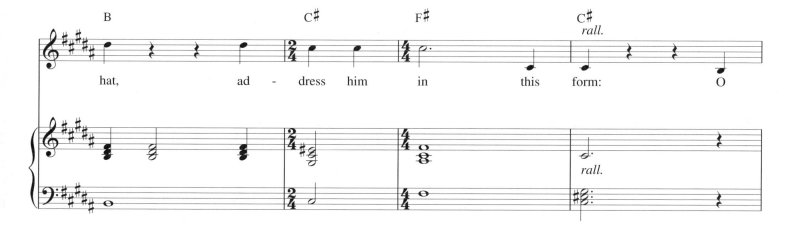

Cat! Be - fore a cat will con - de - scend To treat you as a

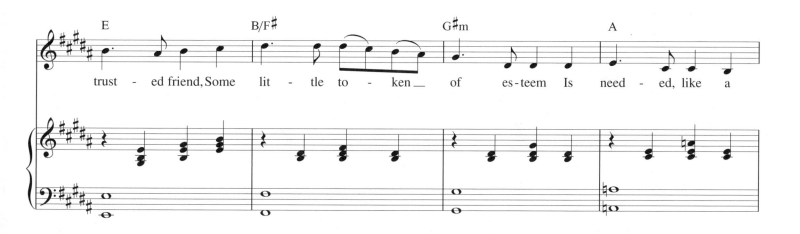

trust - ed friend, Some lit - tle to - ken _ of es - teem Is need - ed, like a

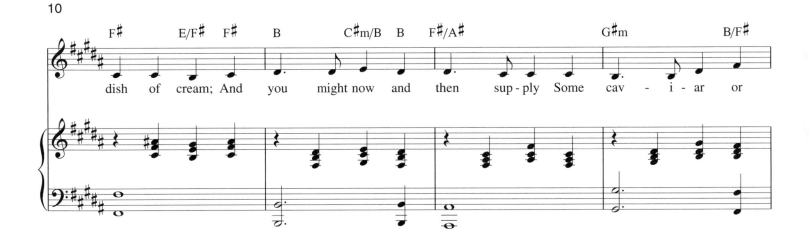

dish of cream; And you might now and then sup-ply Some cav - i - ar or

Strass - burg Pie, Some pot - ted grouse, or ___ sal - mon paste: He's

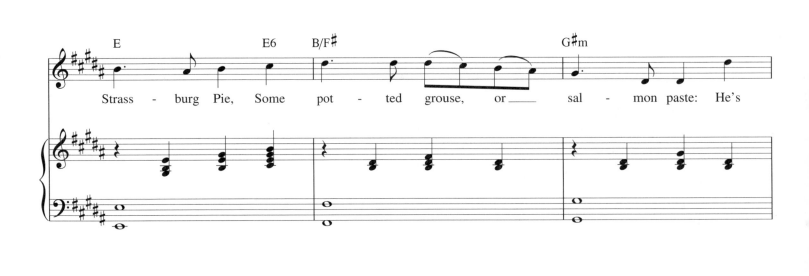

sure to have ___ his ___ per - son - al taste. And so in time ___ you ___

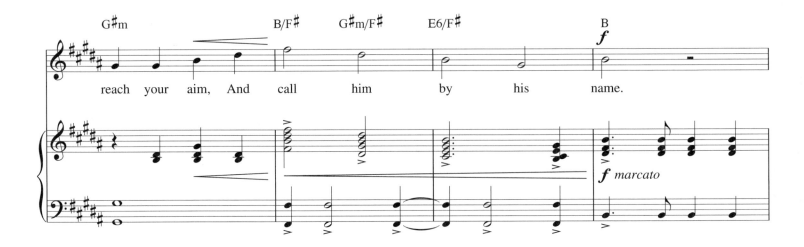

reach your aim, And call him by his name.

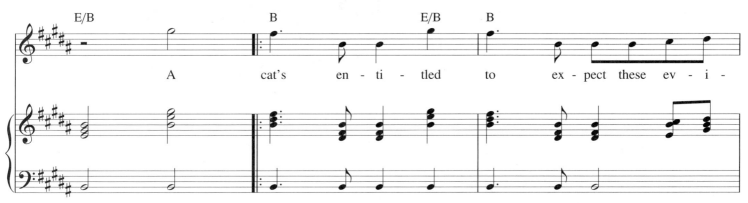

A cat's en-ti-tled to ex-pect these ev-i-

denc-es of re-spect. So this is this, and that is

that: And there's how you ad-dress a

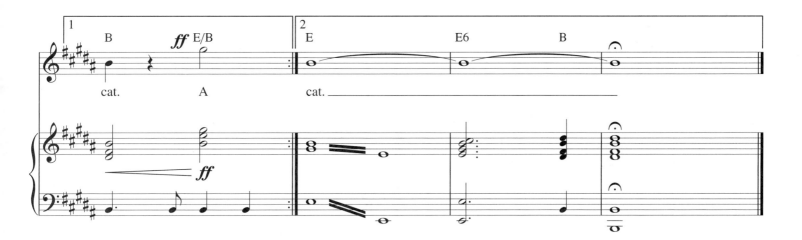

cat. A cat.

# AMIGOS PARA SIEMPRE
## (Friends for Life)
## (The Official Theme of the Barcelona 1992 Games)

Music by ANDREW LLOYD WEBBER
Lyrics by DON BLACK

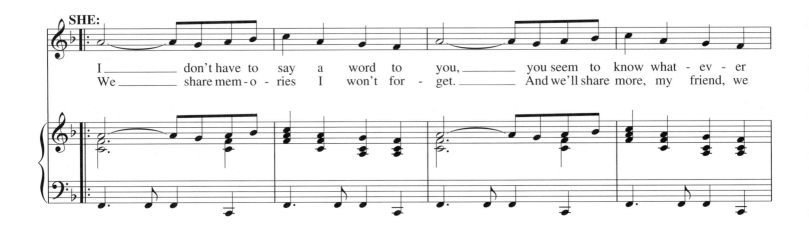

**SHE:**

I _____ don't have to say a word to you,_____ you seem to know what - ev - er
We _____ share mem - o - ries I won't for - get. _____ And we'll share more, my friend, we

mood I'm go - ing through. Feel as though I've known you for - ev - er.
have - n't start - ed yet. Some - thing hap - pens when we're to - geth - er.

HE:

You _____ can look in-to my eyes and see _____ the way I
When _____ I look at you I won-der why _____ there has to

Gm/F

B♭m6/F

feel and how the world is treat-ing me. May-be I have known you for-ev-
come a time when we must say good-bye. I'm a-live when we are to-geth-

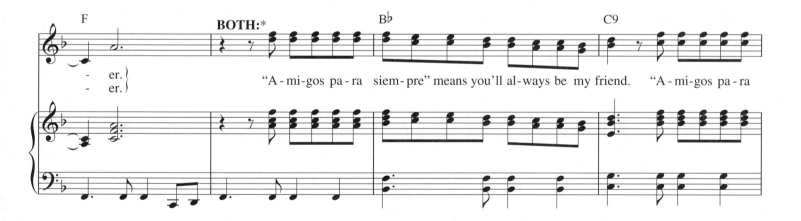

F

BOTH:*

B♭

C9

-er.
-er.

"A-mi-gos pa-ra siem-pre" means you'll al-ways be my friend. "A-mi-gos pa-ra

F

Dm7

Gm

siem-pre" means a love that can-not end. _____ Friends for life, not just a sum-mer or a

* *The top notes are to be sung by the male voice, the bottom by the female voice.*

spring, a - mi - gos pa - ra siem - pre._____ I feel you near me e - ven when we are a -

part. Just know - ing you are in this world can warm my heart._____ Friends for

life, not just a sum - mer or a spring, a - mi - gos pa - ra siem - pre._____

When _____ I look at you I won-der why _____ there has to

come a time when we must say good-bye I'm a-live when we are to-geth - er.

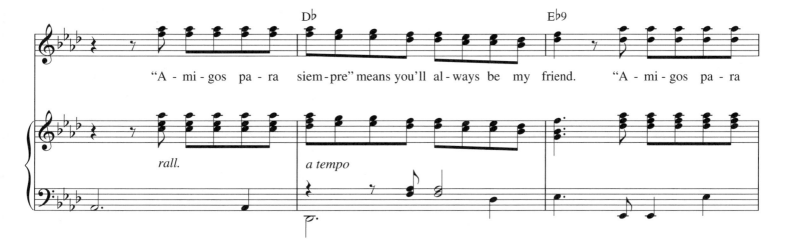

"A - mi - gos pa - ra siem-pre" means you'll al-ways be my friend. "A - mi - gos pa - ra

*rall.*        *a tempo*

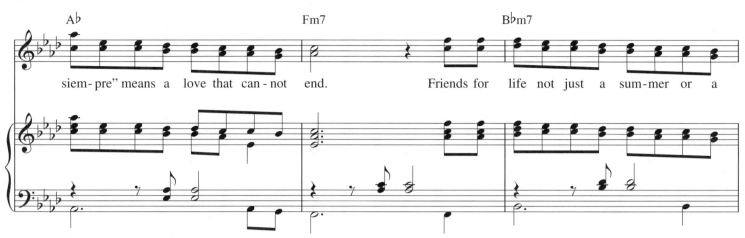

siem-pre" means a love that can-not end. Friends for life not just a sum-mer or a

spring, a - mi-gos pa - ra siem - pre. _____ I feel you

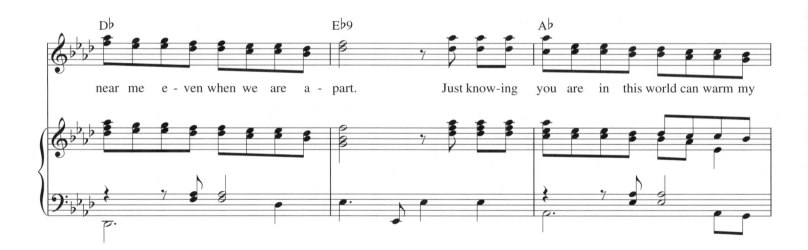

near me e - ven when we are a - part. Just know-ing you are in this world can warm my

heart. Friends for life, not just a sum-mer or a spring, a - mi-gos pa - ra

* *The top notes are to be sung by the female voice, the bottom by the male voice.*

# ALL I ASK OF YOU
## from *The Phantom of the Opera*

Music by ANDREW LLOYD WEBBER
Lyrics by CHARLES HART
Additional Lyrics by RICHARD STILGOE

19

here, with you, be-side you, to guard you and to guide you.

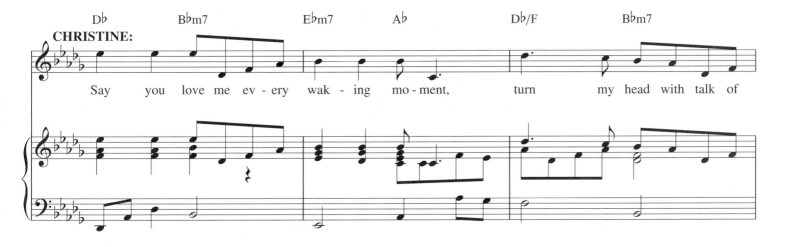

**CHRISTINE:**
Say you love me ev-ery wak-ing mo-ment, turn my head with talk of

sum-mer-time. Say you need me with you now and al-ways;

prom-ise me that all you say is true, that's all I ask of

**RAOUL:** Let me be your shel-ter, let me be your light; you're safe, no one will find you your you.

fears are far be-hind you. **CHRISTINE:** All I want is free-dom, a world with no more night; and

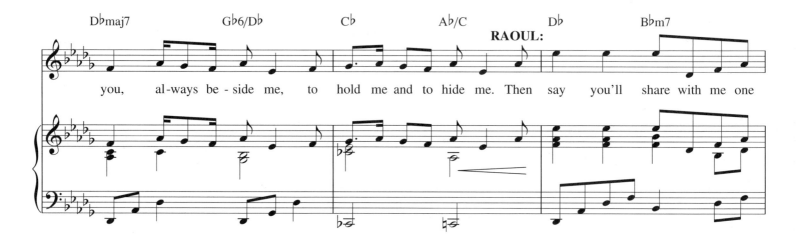

you, al-ways be-side me, to hold me and to hide me. **RAOUL:** Then say you'll share with me one

love, one life-time; let me lead you from your sol-i-tude. _

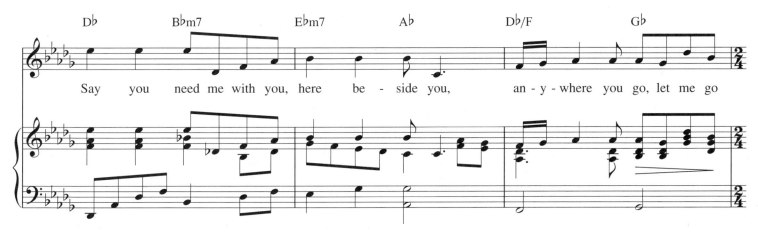

Say you need me with you, here be - side you, an - y - where you go, let me go too.

too. Chris - tine, — that's all I ask of you.

CHRISTINE:
Say you'll share with me one

love, one life - time; say the word and I will fol-low you. —

TOGETHER:
Share each day with me, each night, each morn - ing. Say you love me!

CHRISTINE:
RAOUL:
You know I

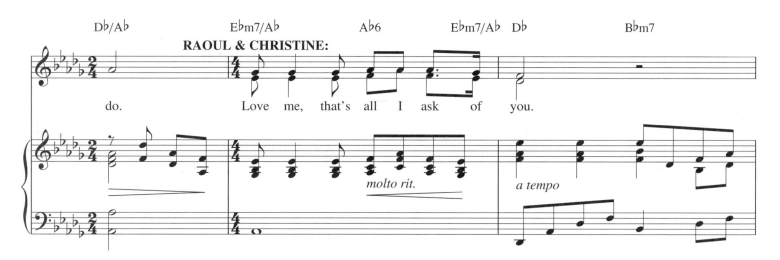

**RAOUL & CHRISTINE:**

do. Love me, that's all I ask of you.

*molto rit.* *a tempo*

**CHRISTINE & RAOUL:**

An - y - where you go, let me go

*f* *ff largo*

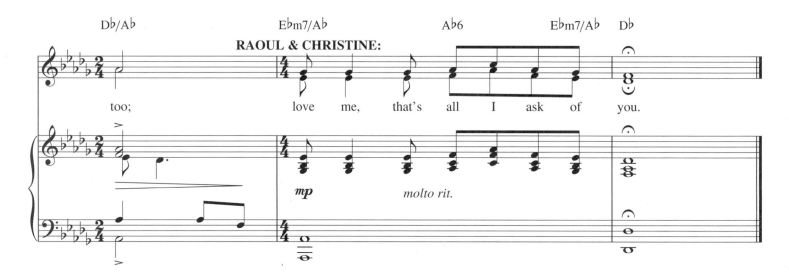

**RAOUL & CHRISTINE:**

too; love me, that's all I ask of you.

*mp* *molto rit.*

# ANY DREAM WILL DO

## from *Joseph and the Amazing Technicolor® Dreamcoat*

Music by ANDREW LLOYD WEBBER
Lyrics by TIM RICE

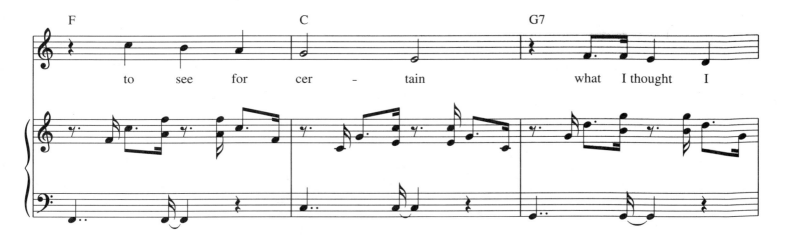

knew.              Far  far  a - way             some - one  was

weep -      ing,           but  the  world  was  sleep -     ing,

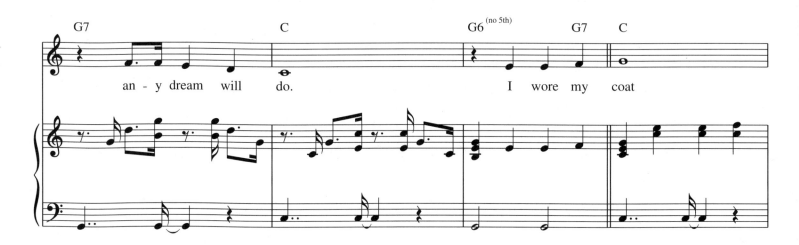

an - y  dream  will   do.               I  wore  my  coat

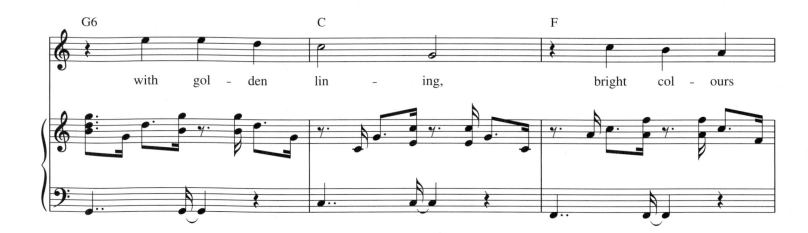

with  gol - den  lin -    ing,          bright  col - ours

shin - ing wonderful and new.

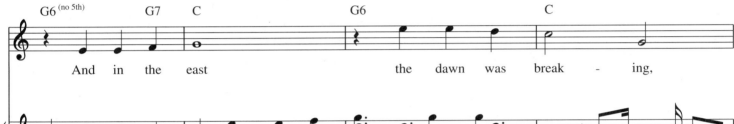

And in the east the dawn was break - ing,

and the world was wak - ing, an - y dream will do.

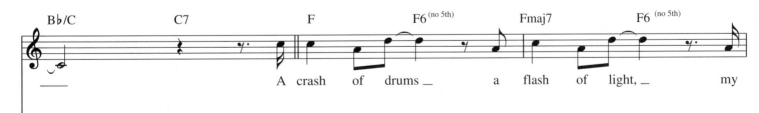

A crash of drums _ a flash of light, _ my

_mf_

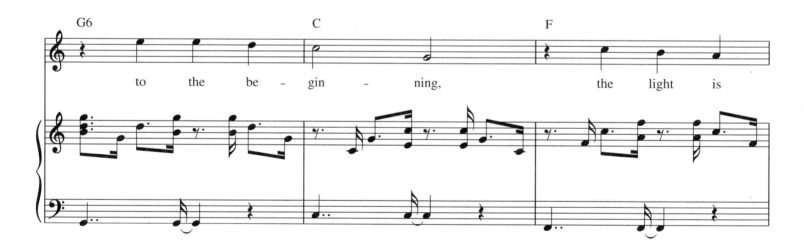

the world and I, we are still wait - ing,

still hes - i - tat - ing an - y dream will do,

an - y dream will do,

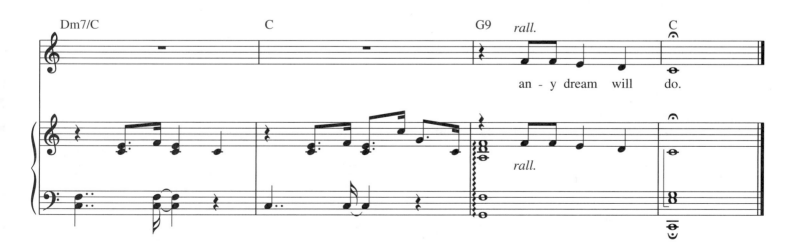

an - y dream will do.

# THE BALLAD OF BILLY M'CAW
## from *Cats*

Music by ANDREW LLOYD WEBBER
Text by T.S. ELIOT

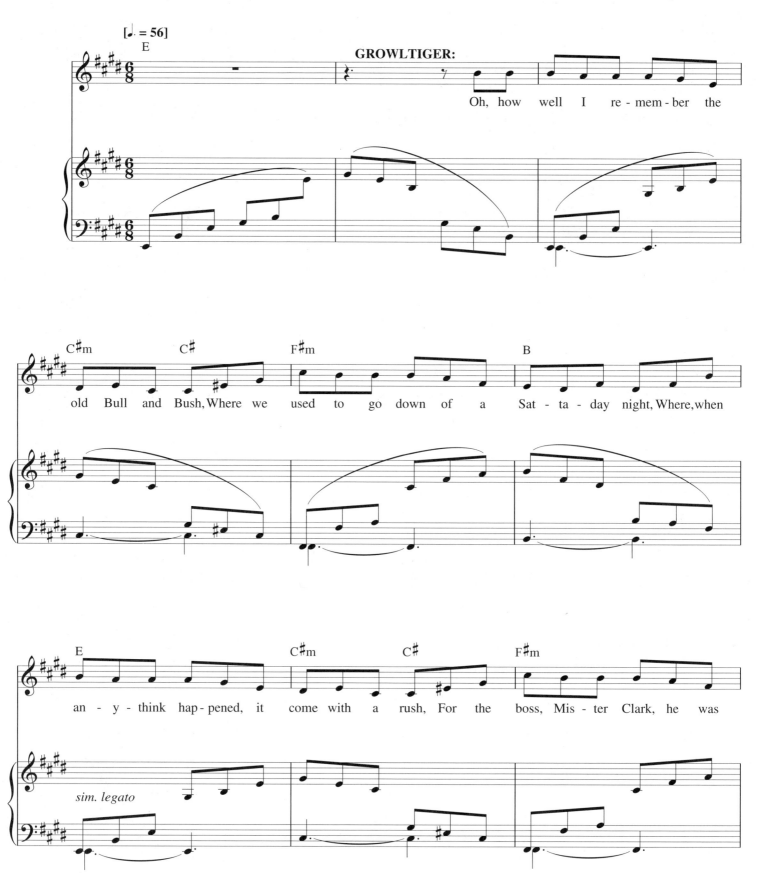

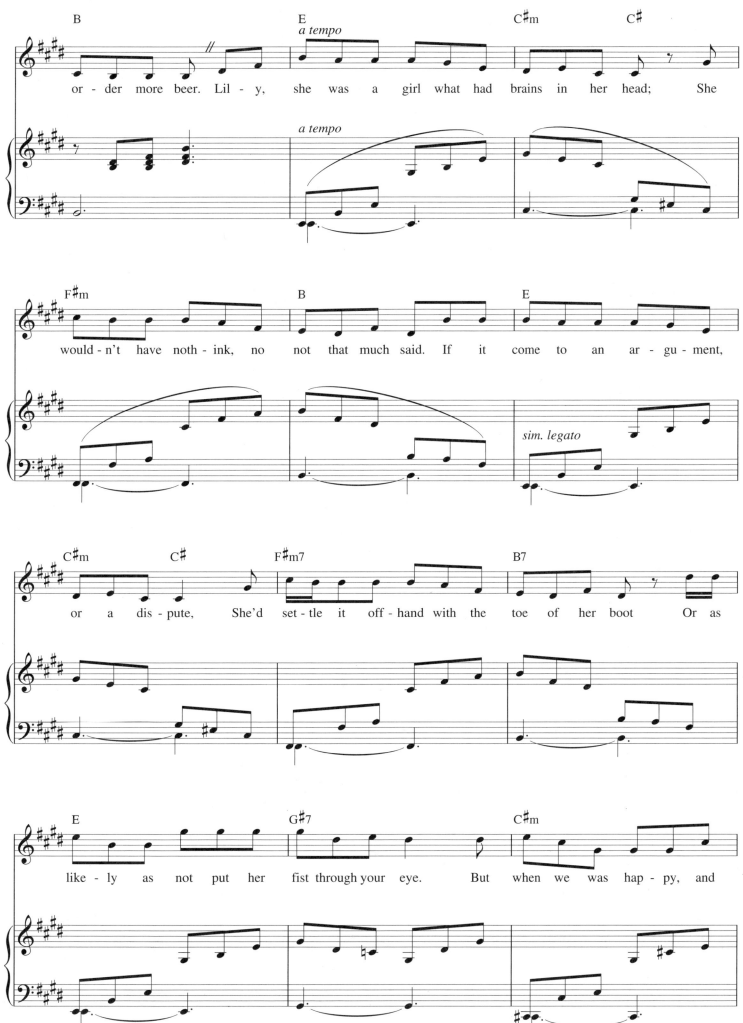

just a bit dry, Or when we was thirs-ty, and just a bit sad, She would

rap on the bar with that cork-screw she had And say, "Bil - ly! Bil - ly M'-
"Bil - ly! Bil - ly M'-

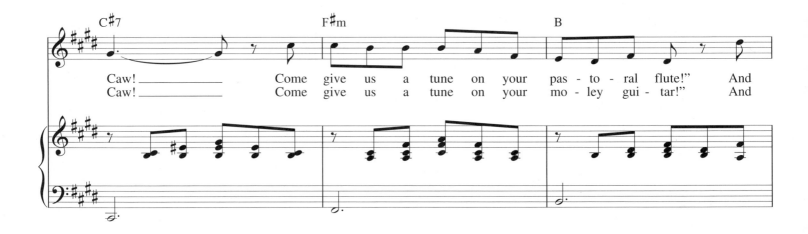

Caw! _____ Come give us a tune on your pas - to - ral flute!" And
Caw! _____ Come give us a tune on your mo - ley gui - tar!" And

Bil - ly'd strike up on his pas - to - ral flute, and Bil - ly'd strike up on his
Bil - ly'd strike up on his mo - ley gui - tar, and Bil - ly'd strike up on his

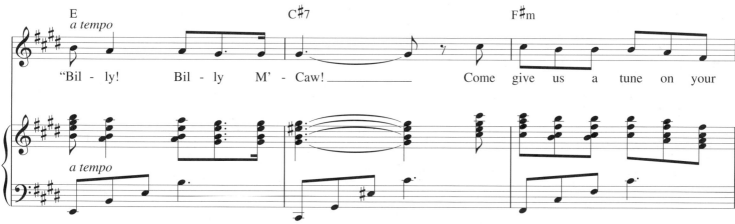

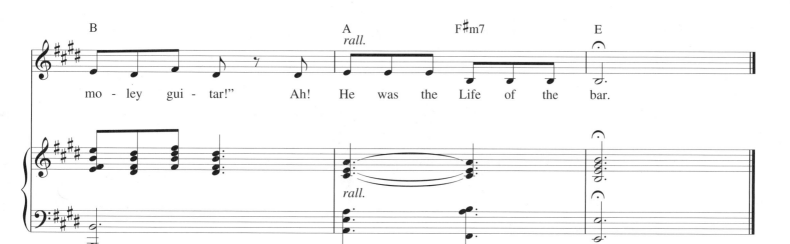

# BENJAMIN CALYPSO

## from *Joseph and the Amazing Technicolor® Dreamcoat*

Music by ANDREW LLOYD WEBBER
Lyrics by TIM RICE

I hear de steel drums sing dere song, _ Dey're sing-in' man you know you
Sure as de tide wash de gold-en sand, _ Ben-ja - min is an

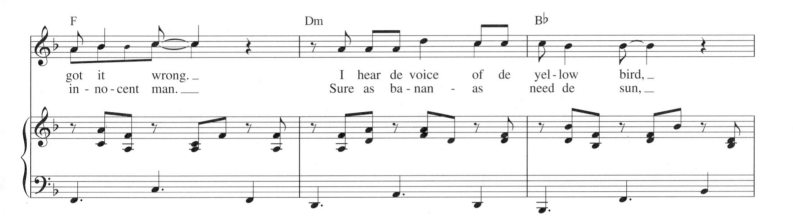

got it wrong. _ I hear de voice of de yel-low bird, _
in - no - cent man. ___ Sure as ba-nan - as need de sun, _

Sing-in' in de tree, dis is quite ab - surd. _ Oh yes, ___ it's true, _
We are de crim-i - nal guil-ty ones. _ Oh no, ___ not he, ___

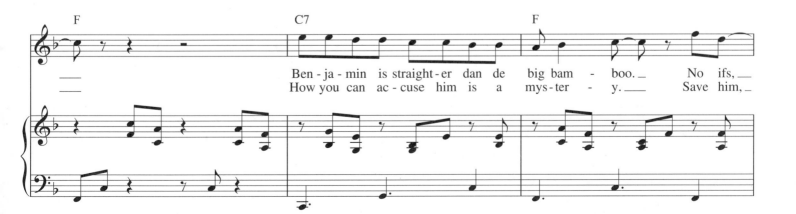

Ben-ja - min is straight-er dan de big bam - boo. _ No ifs, ___
How you can ac - cuse him is a mys-ter - y. _ Save him, _

no buts, ___ Ben-ja-min is hon-est as
take me, ___ Ben-ja-min is straight-er dan de

co-co-nuts. ___
tall palm tree. ___ La la la ___ la la la la la, ___

La la la ___ la la la la, La la la ___ la la la

la la la, ___ La la la ___ la la la la.

# CLOSE EVERY DOOR

## from *Joseph and the Amazing Technicolor® Dreamcoat*

Music by ANDREW LLOYD WEBBER
Lyrics by TIM RICE

Espressivo

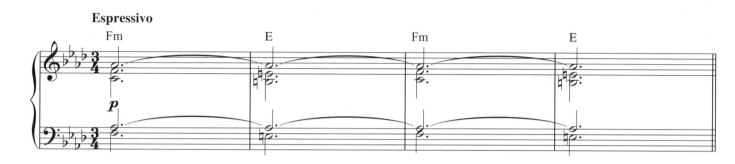

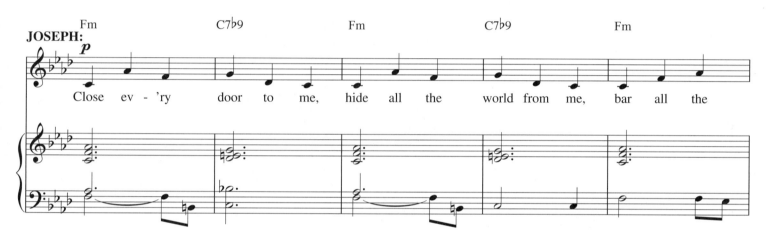

JOSEPH:

Close ev-'ry door to me, hide all the world from me, bar all the

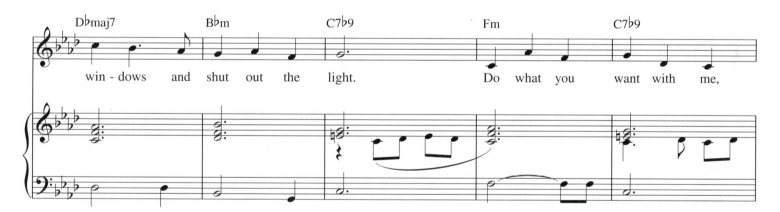

win - dows and shut out the light. Do what you want with me,

hate me and laugh at me, dark - en my day - time and tor - ture my

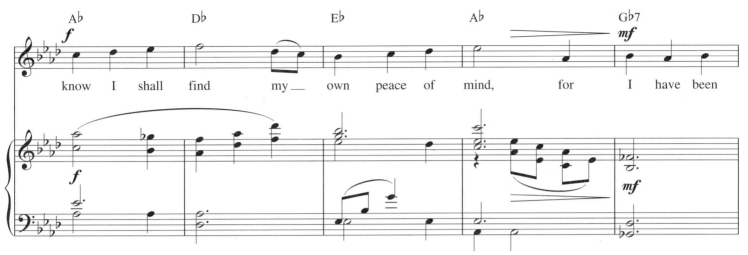

know I shall find my own peace of mind, for I have been

prom - ised a land of my own.

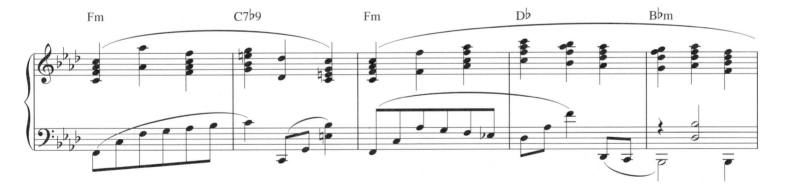

Just give me a num - ber in - stead of my

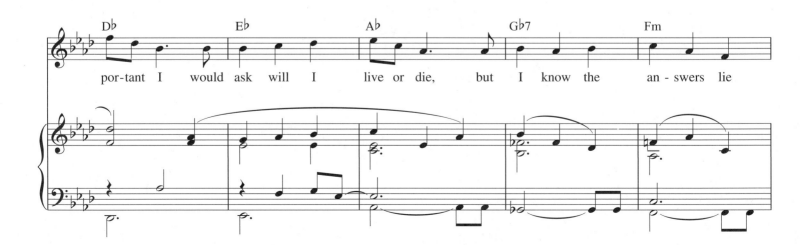

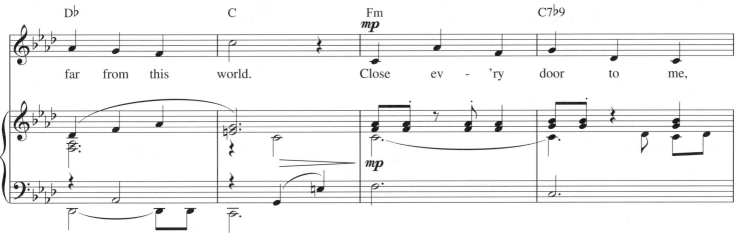

far from this world. Close ev - 'ry door to me,

keep those I love from me, chil - dren of Is - rael are

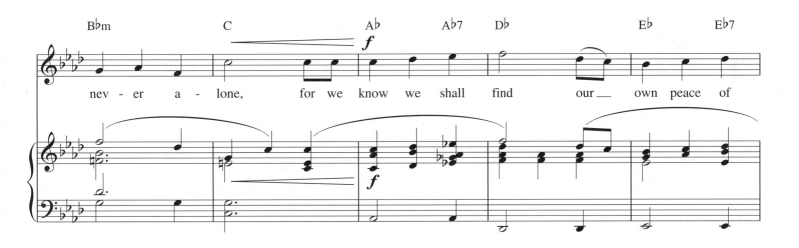

nev - er a - lone, for we know we shall find our___ own peace of

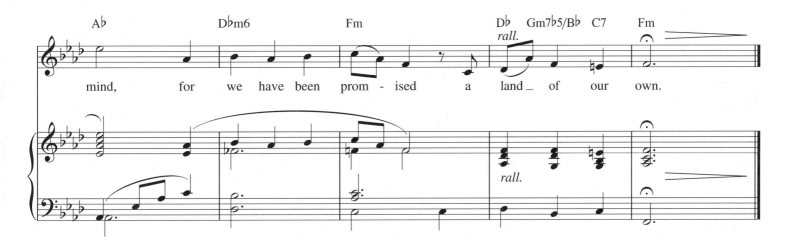

mind, for we have been prom - ised a land___ of our own.

# EVERMORE WITHOUT YOU
## from *The Woman in White*

Music by ANDREW LLOYD WEBBER
Lyrics by DAVID ZIPPEL

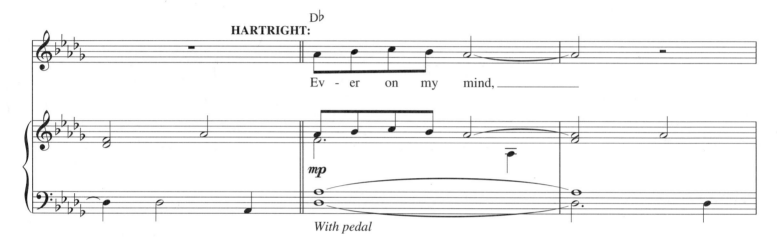

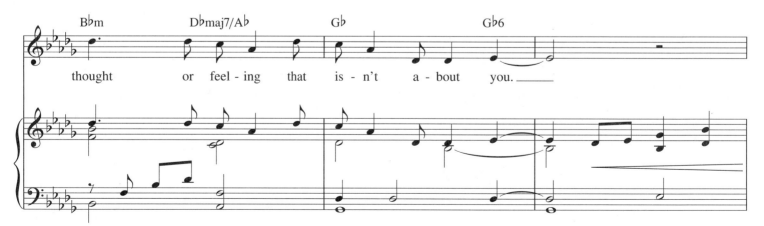

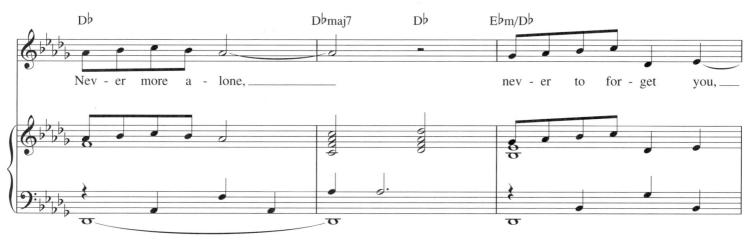

Nev - er more a - lone, _____ nev - er to for - get you, ___

___ not when my life was changed for - ev - er the

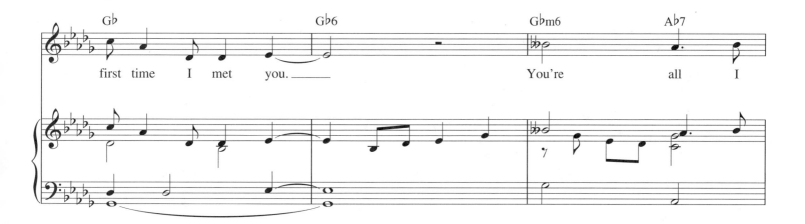

first time I met you. _____ You're all I

know, and though I've lost you, you're some - one I can't let

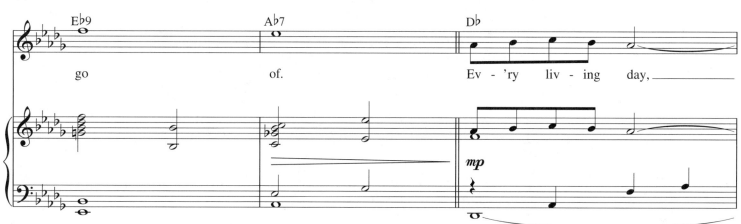

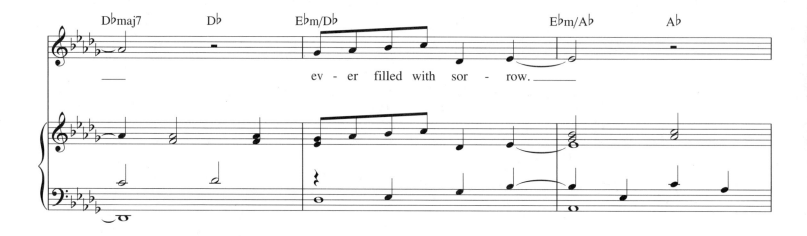

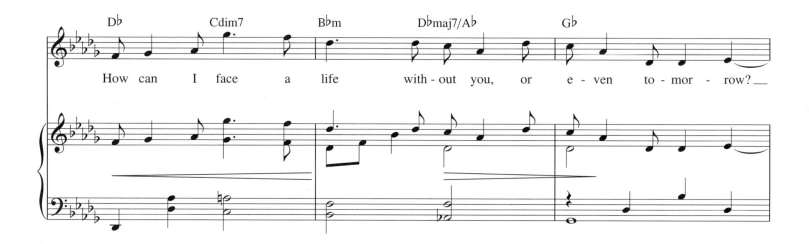

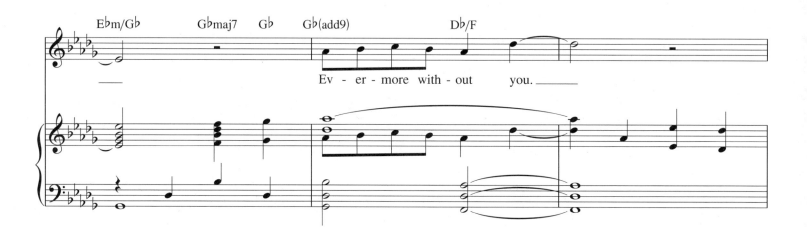

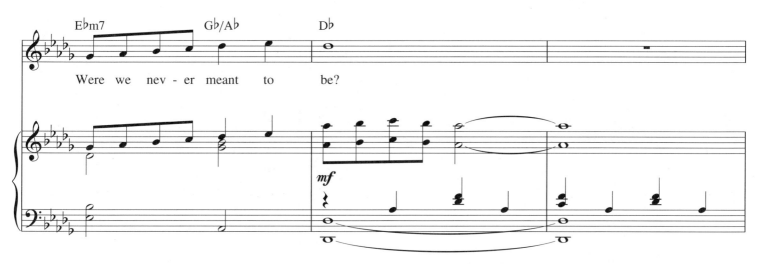

Were we nev - er meant to be?

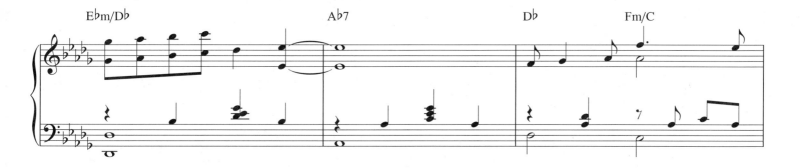

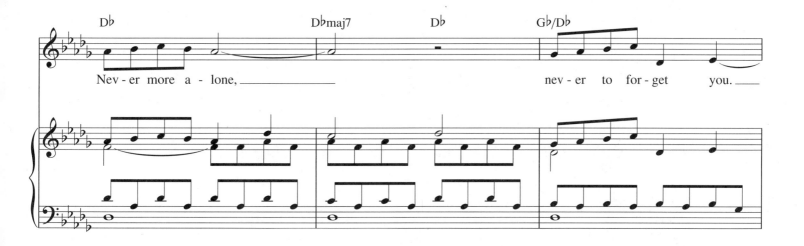

Nev - er more a - lone, _____ nev - er to for - get you. ____

Not when my life was changed for - ev - er the

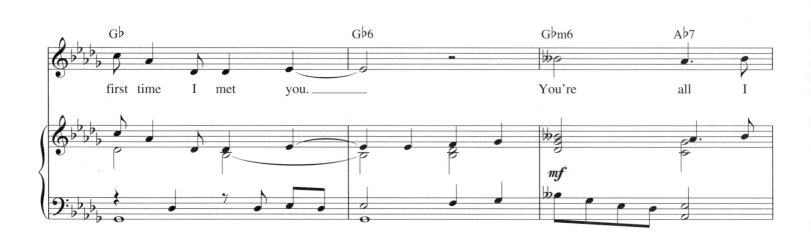

first time I met you. _____ You're all I

know and though I've lost you, you're some - one I can't let

go of. Ev - 'ry liv - ing day, _____

ev - er filled with sor - row. _____

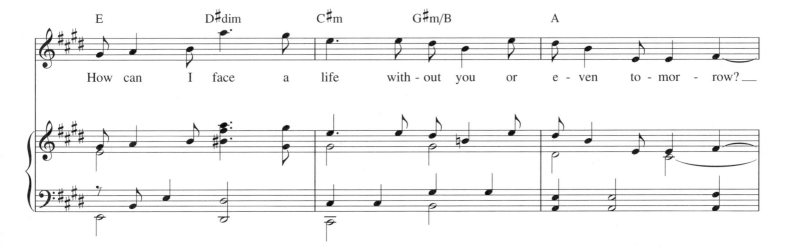

How can I face a life with - out you or e - ven to - mor - row? __

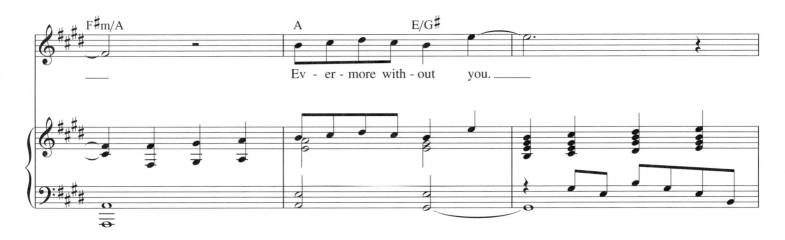

_____ Ev - er - more with - out you. _____

Were we nev - er meant to be?

# THE GREATEST STAR OF ALL
## from *Sunset Boulevard*

Music by ANDREW LLOYD WEBBER
Lyrics by DON BLACK and CHRISTOPHER HAMPTON,
with contributions by Amy Powers

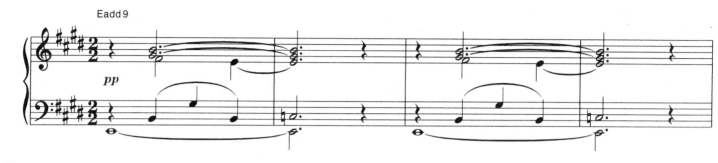

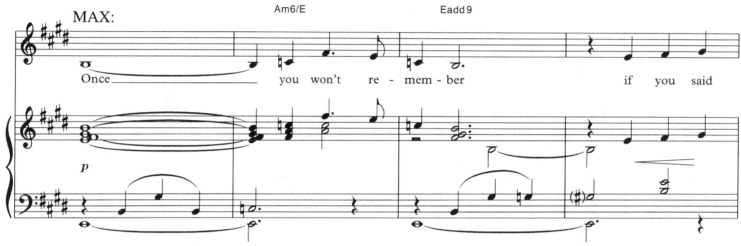

MAX:

Once_____ you won't re-mem-ber if you said

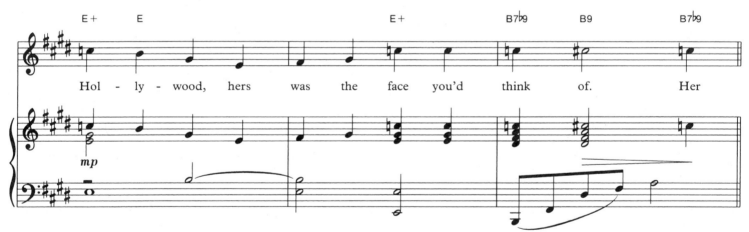

Hol-ly-wood, hers was the face you'd think of. Her

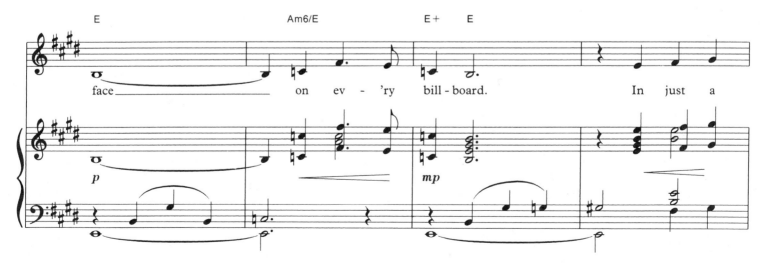

face_____ on ev-'ry bill-board. In just a

sin - gle week she'd get ten thou - sand let - ters.

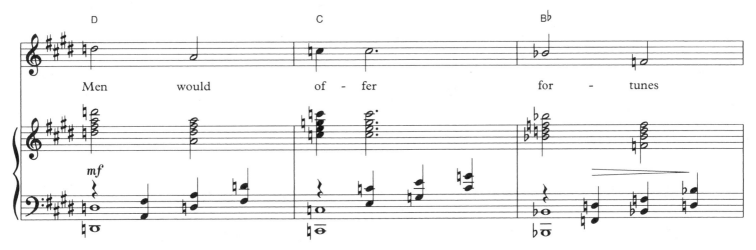

Men would of - fer for - tunes

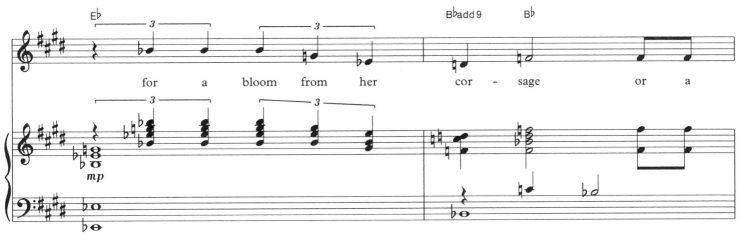

for a bloom from her cor - sage or a

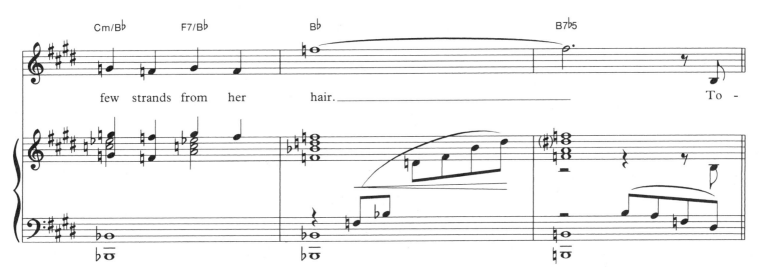

few strands from her hair._____ To -

-day _____ she's half for - got - ten,

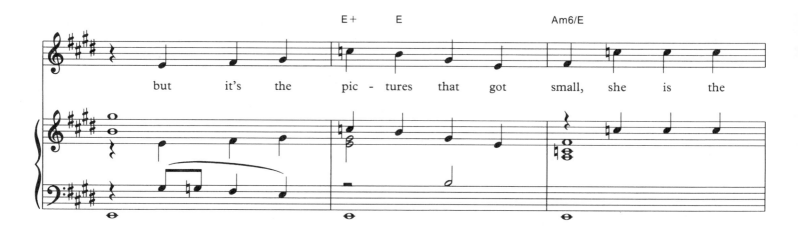

but it's the pic - tures that got small, she is the

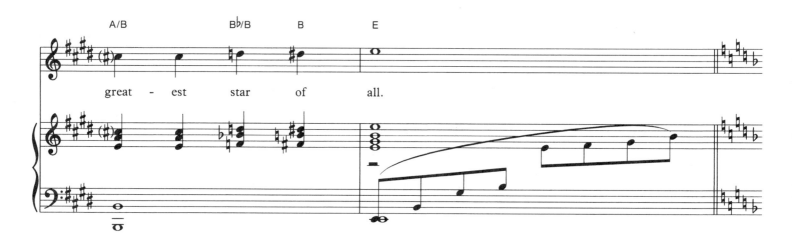

great - est star of all.

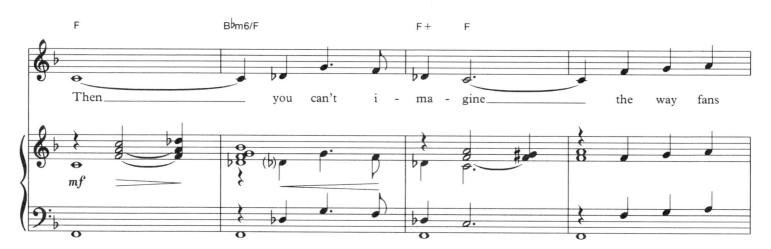

Then _____ you can't i - ma - gine _____ the way fans

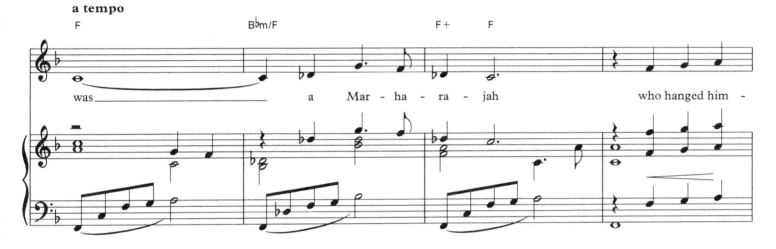

-side that flick - er - ing light beam is a

youth which can - not fade._____ Ma -

-dame's\_\_\_\_\_ a liv - ing le - gend, I've seen so ma - ny i - dols

fall, she is the great - est star of all.

# GUS: THE THEATRE CAT

## from *Cats*

Music by ANDREW LLOYD WEBBER
Text by T.S. ELIOT

*The "Gus" sections may be sung in character, distinguishing them from the "Solo" sections.

palm - i - est days. For he once was a Star of the high-est de - gree: He has
likes to re - late his suc-cess on the Halls, Where the

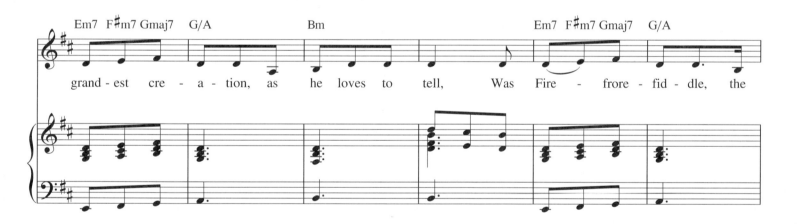

act - ed with Irv - ing, he's act - ed with Tree. And he
Gal - ler - y once gave him sev - en cat - calls. But his

grand - est cre - a - tion, as he loves to tell, Was Fire - frore - fid - dle, the

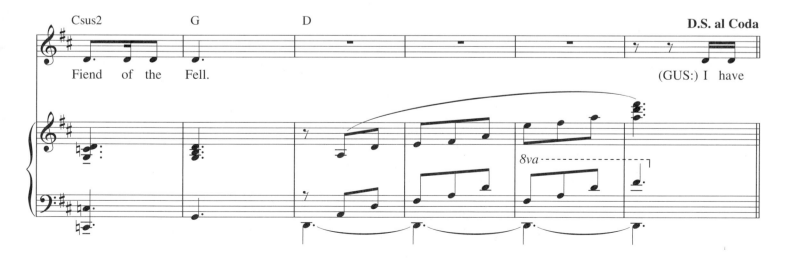

Fiend of the Fell.

**D.S. al Coda**

(GUS:) I have

**CODA**

Bm   Em7 F#m7 Gmaj7 G/A   Bm

cat. But my grand - est cre - a - tion, as his - t'ry will tell, Was

Em7 F#m7 Gmaj7 G/A   Csus2   G/B   D

Fire - frore - fid - dle, the Fiend of the Fell.

**Più mosso**

C#/A   D

(SOLO:) Then, if some - one will give him a tooth - ful of gin, He will

A7sus/E   A7   D   C#/A

tell how he once played a part in "East Lynne". At a Shake - speare per - for - mance he

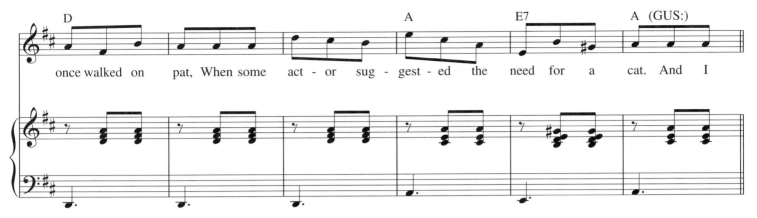

once walked on pat, When some act - or sug - gest - ed the need for a cat. And I

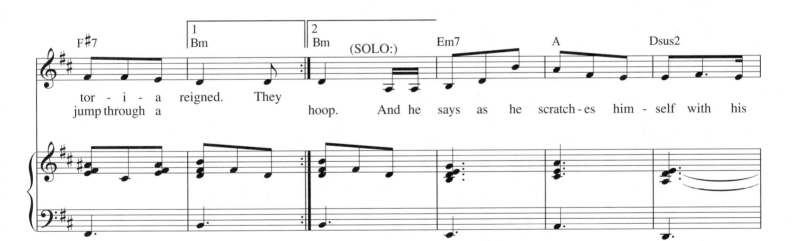

**Meno mosso**

say: Now, these kit - tens, they do not get trained As we did in the days when Vic -
nev - er get drilled in a reg - u - lar troupe, And they think they are smart, just to

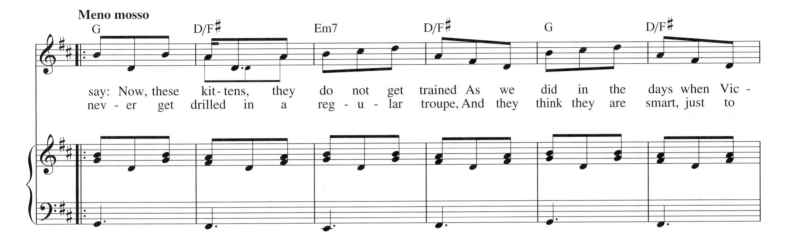

tor - i - a reigned. They
jump through a hoop. And he says as he scratch - es him - self with his

claws: Well, the Thea - tre is cer - tain - ly not what it was. These mod - ern pro -

duc - tions are all ver - y well, But there's noth - ing to e - qual, from what I hear

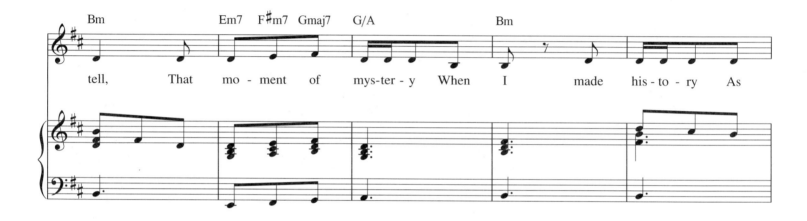

tell, That mo - ment of mys-ter - y When I made his-to-ry As

Fire - frore - fid - dle, the Fiend of the Fell.

And I once crossed the stage on a tel - e - graph wire, To

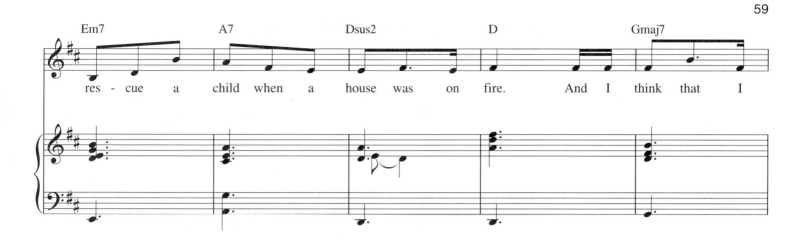

res - cue a child when a house was on fire. And I think that I

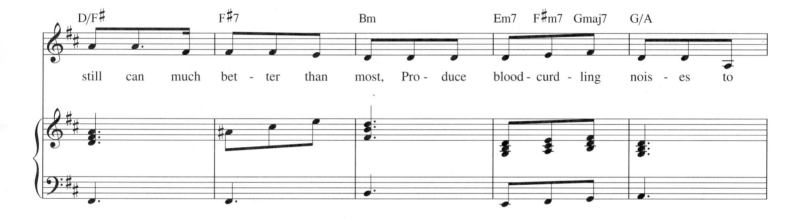

still can much bet - ter than most, Pro - duce blood - curd - ling nois - es to

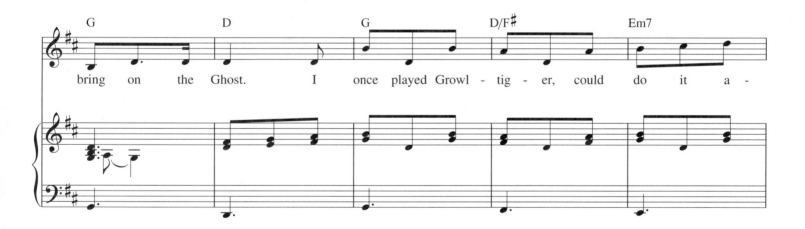

bring on the Ghost. I once played Growl - tig - er, could do it a -

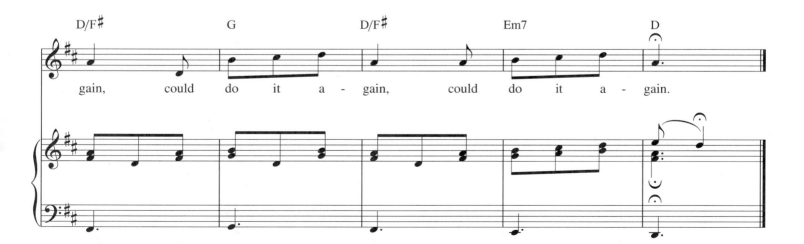

gain, could do it a - gain, could do it a - gain.

# HALF A MOMENT
## from By Jeeves

Words by ALAN AYCKBOURN
Music by ANDREW LLOYD WEBBER

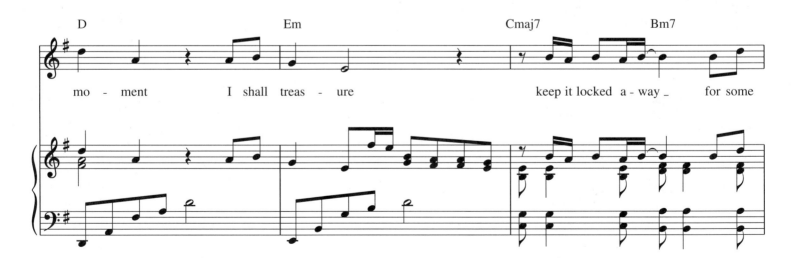

fu - ture rain - y day. _ Should you leave me _____ with just this mo - ment, in my

mind I shall cap - ture it a - new. _____ Like some pic - ture ta - ken in my

child - hood, half a mo - ment spent with you.

Half a

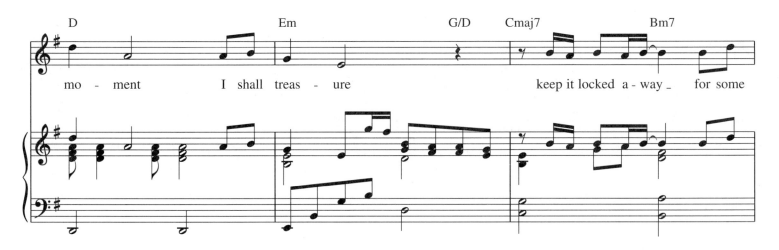

Count - less viv - id mem - o - ries spin be-fore my view. Like some toy ka - lei - do-scope

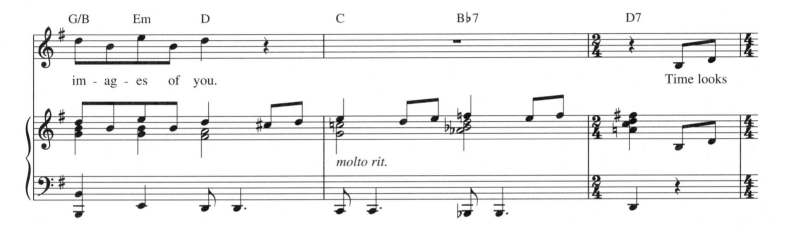

im - ag - es of you. Time looks

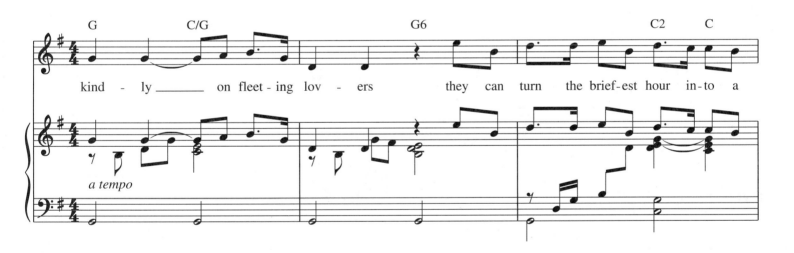

kind - ly _____ on fleet - ing lov - ers they can turn the brief-est hour in-to a

day, turn a mo - ment to a life - time

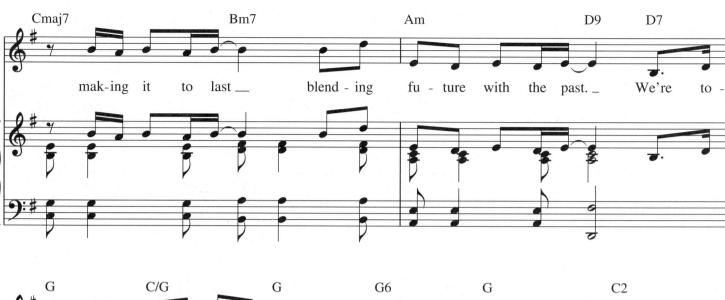

mak-ing it to last __ blend-ing fu-ture with the past. __ We're to-

geth - er _____ what else can mat - ter e - ven though half a mo-ment is too

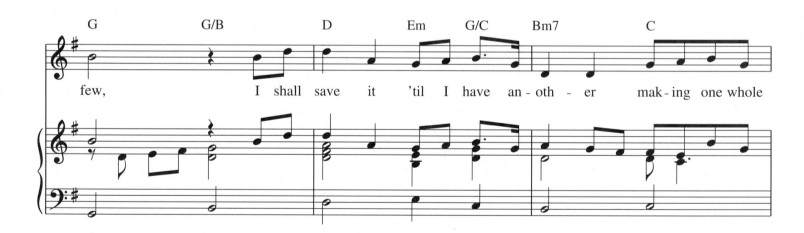

few, I shall save it 'til I have an-oth - er mak-ing one whole

mo - ment filled with you.

# HIGH FLYING, ADORED
### from *Evita*

Words by TIM RICE
Music by ANDREW LLOYD WEBBER

*The right hand part of piano is a simple suggestion of the kind of improvisation that is appropriate in this song.*

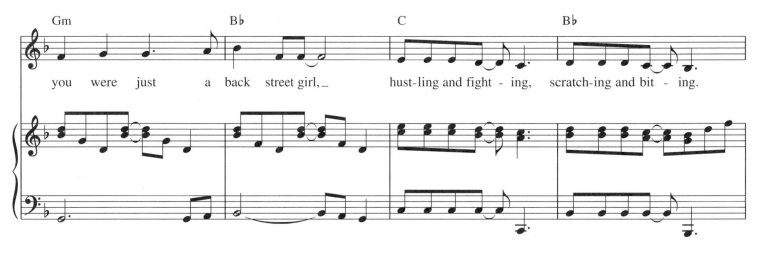

you were just a back street girl, __ hust-ling and fight - ing, scratch-ing and bit - ing.

High fly-ing, a - dored. __ Did you be - lieve in your wild - est mo - ments

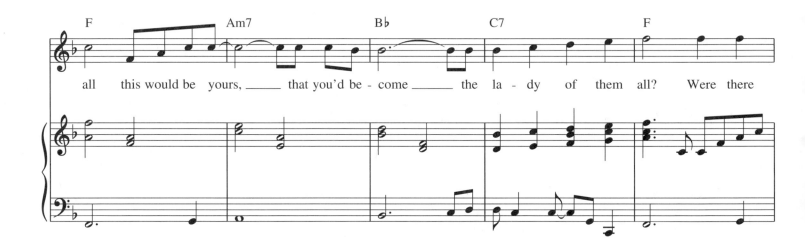

all this would be yours, _____ that you'd be - come _____ the la - dy of them all? Were there

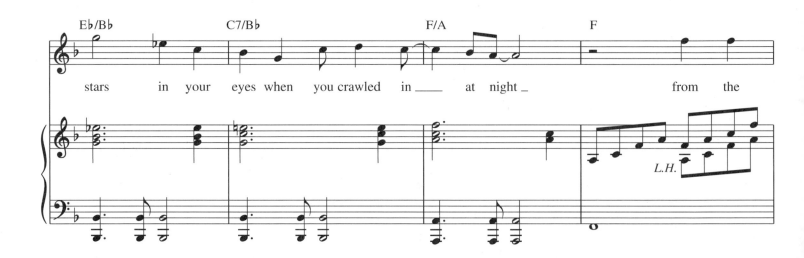

stars in your eyes when you crawled in ____ at night _ from the

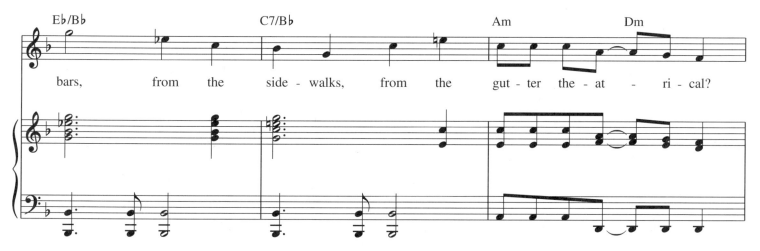

bars, from the side - walks, from the gut - ter the - at - ri - cal?

Don't look down, it's a long, long way to

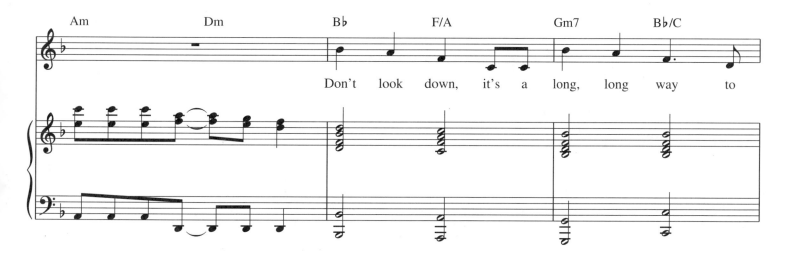

fall.

High fly - ing, a - dored. _____ What hap-pens now? ____ Where do you go from here? _ For

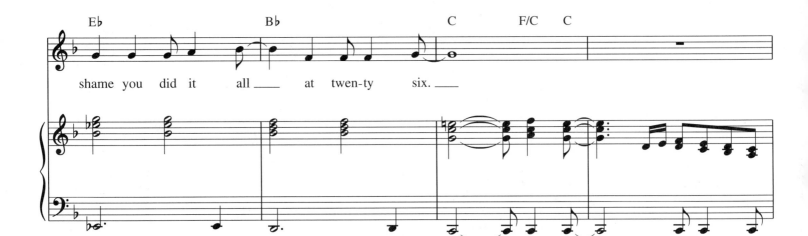

some-one on top of the world __ the view's not ex - act - ly clear. __ A

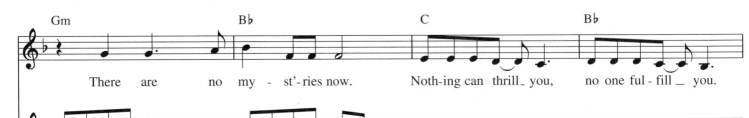

shame you did it all __ at twen-ty six. __

There are no my - st'-ries now. Noth-ing can thrill __ you, no one ful - fill __ you.

High fly-ing, a - dored. __ I hope you come to terms with bore - dom.

So fa-mous so eas - i - ly, so soon ___ is not the wis - est thing to be. You won't

care if they love you, it's been done ___ be - fore. ___ You'll des -

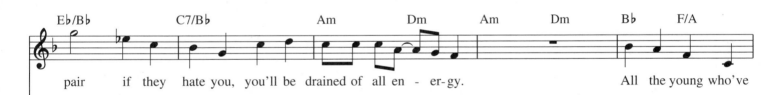

pair if they hate you, you'll be drained of all en - er - gy. All the young who've

made it will a - gree. ___

# HEAVEN ON THEIR MINDS
## from *Jesus Christ Superstar*

Words by TIM RICE
Music by ANDREW LLOYD WEBBER

**Moderate Rock tempo**

Je - sus! _____ You've

start-ed to be - lieve The things they say of you You real-ly do be - lieve This

talk of God is true _____ And

all the good you've done will soon be swept a - way, You've be-gun to mat-ter more \_ than \_

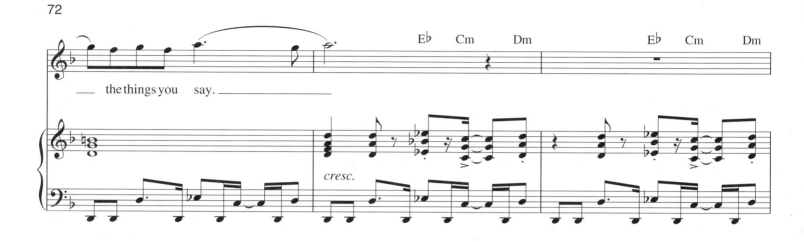

_the things you say._

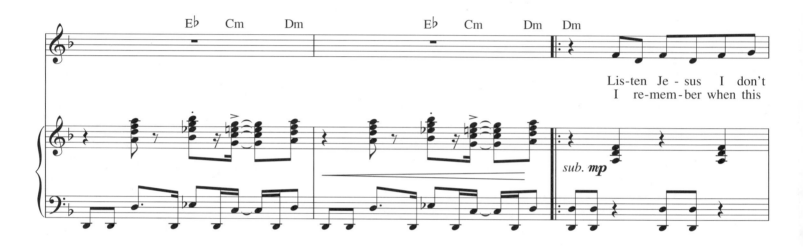

Lis-ten Je - sus I don't
I re-mem - ber when this

like what I see ___ All I ask is that you lis - ten to me
whole thing be - gan ___ No talk of God then we called you a man

And re - mem - ber— I've been your right hand man ___ all a - long. ___
And be - lieve me— my ad - mi - ra - tion for you has - n't died ___

You have set them all on fire
But ev-'ry word you say to-day

They think they've
Gets twist - ed

found the new Mes - si - ah
'round some oth - er way

And they'll hurt you when they find they're
And they'll hurt you if they think you've

wrong.

lied.

Naz - a - reth your fa - mous son should have stayed a great un-known

Like his fa - ther carv - ing wood— He'd have made good __ Ta - bles, chairs and oak - en chests

would have suit - ed Je - sus best He'd have caused no - bod - y harm— no - one a - larm __

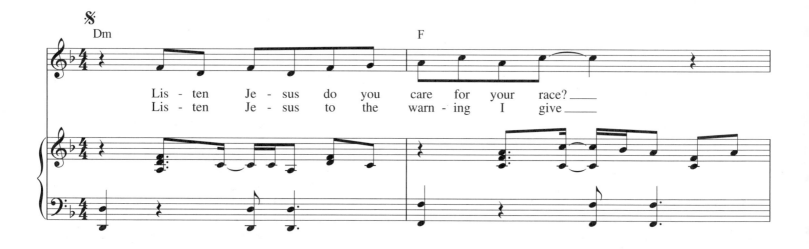

Lis - ten Je - sus do you care for your race?__
Lis - ten Je - sus to the warn - ing I give __

Don't you see we must keep in our place?
Please re - mem - ber that I want us to live

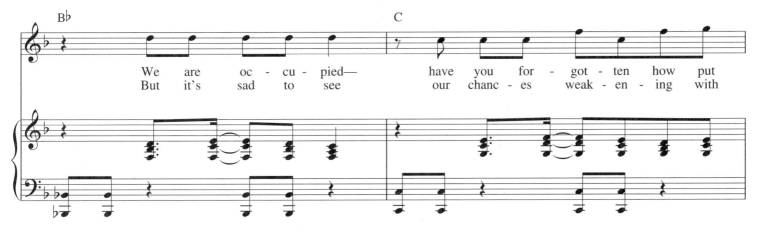

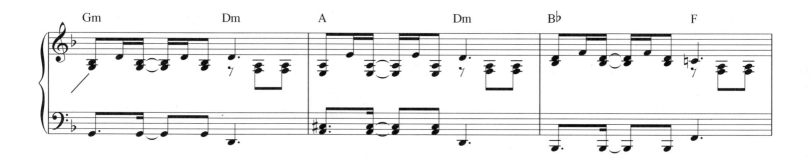

**D.S. al Coda**

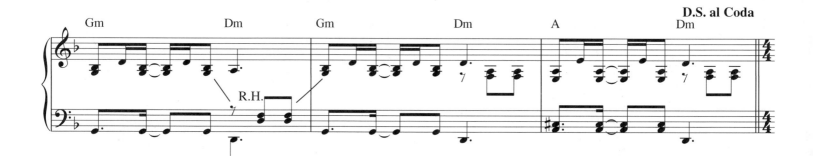

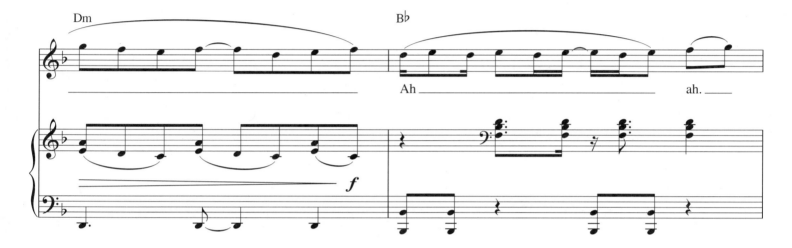

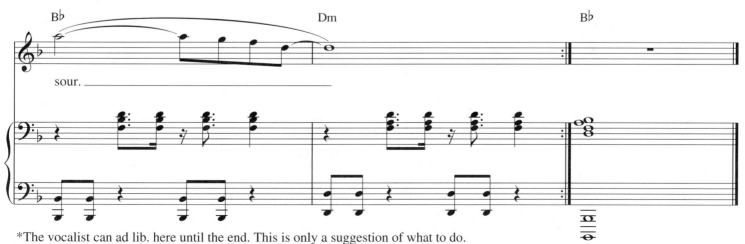

*The vocalist can ad lib. here until the end. This is only a suggestion of what to do.

# I ONLY WANT TO SAY
## (Gethsemane)
### from *Jesus Christ Superstar*

Words by TIM RICE
Music by ANDREW LLOYD WEBBER

**Moderately, not too fast**

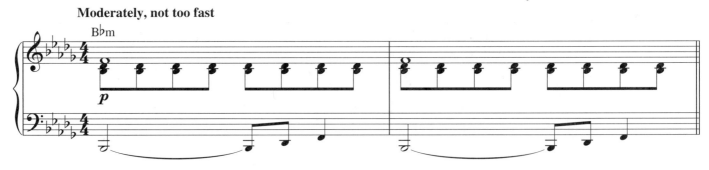

JESUS:
I on-ly want to say, if there is a

way, take this cup a-way from me, for

I don't want to taste its poi-son. Feel it burn me.

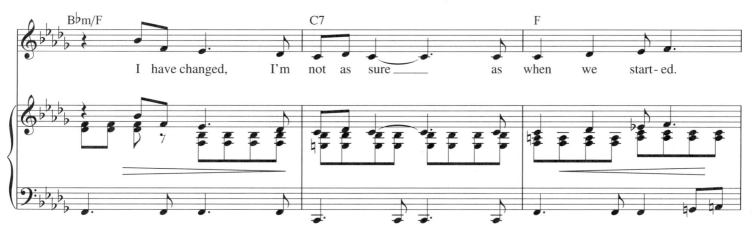

I have changed, I'm not as sure ____ as when we start-ed.

Then I was in - spired. Now I'm sad and

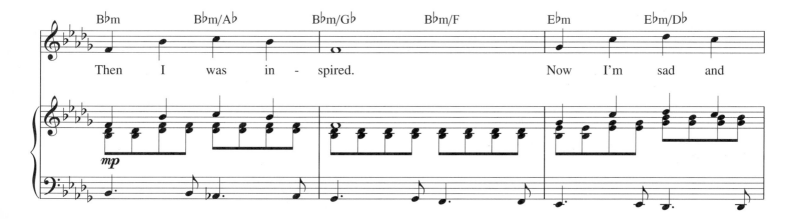

tired. Lis - ten, sure - ly I've ex - ceed - ed

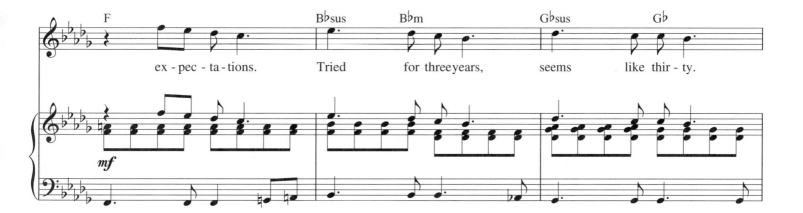

ex - pec - ta - tions. Tried for three years, seems like thir - ty.

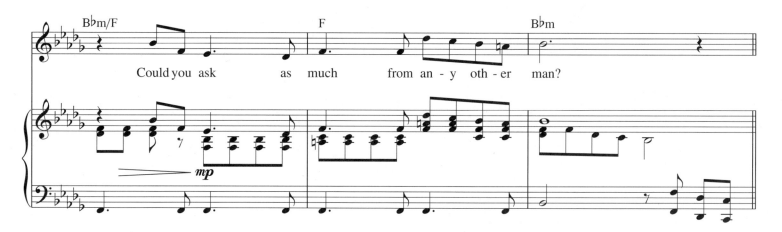

Could you ask as much from an - y oth - er man?

But if I die, see the sa - ga through and do the

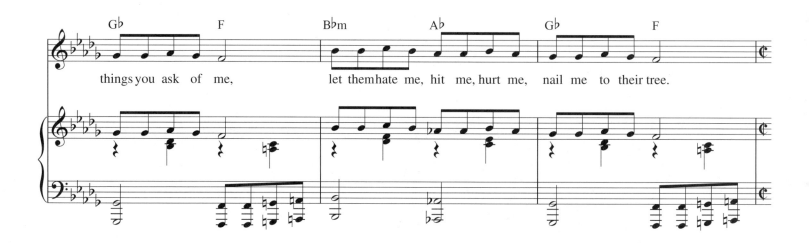

things you ask of me, let them hate me, hit me, hurt me, nail me to their tree.

I'd wan - na know, I'd wan - na know my God. I'd wan - na know, I'd wan -

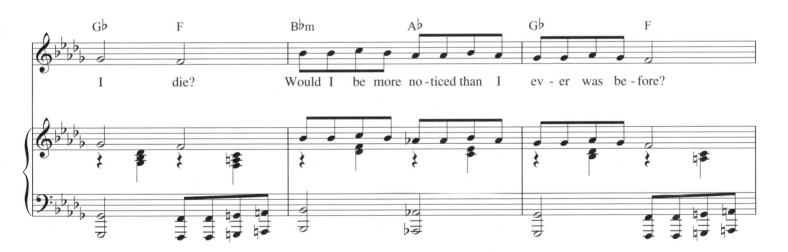

want-ing me to die. You're far too keen on where and how and not so hot on why.

Al - right I'll die! Just watch

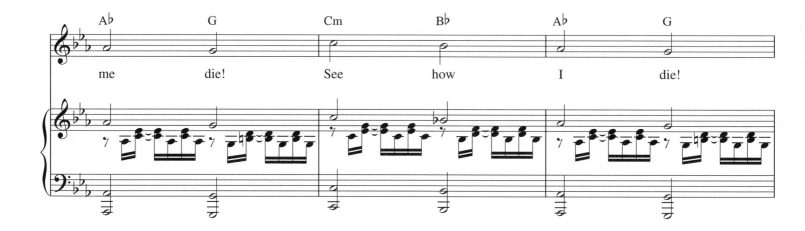

me die! See how I die!

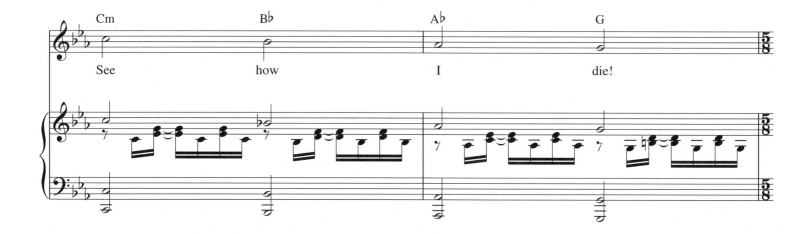

See how I die!

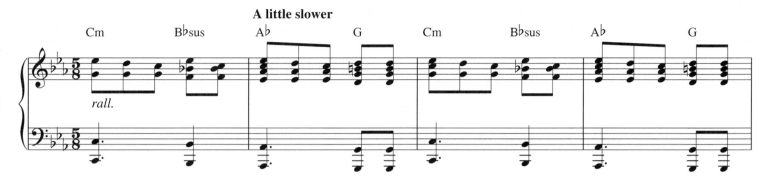

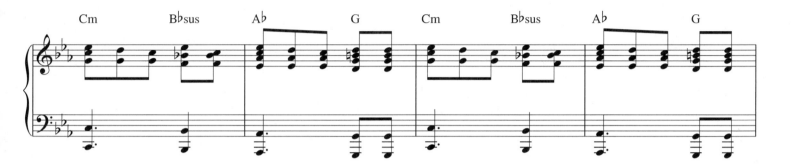

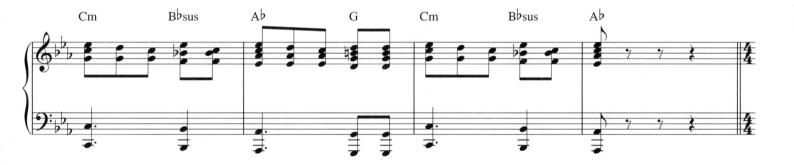

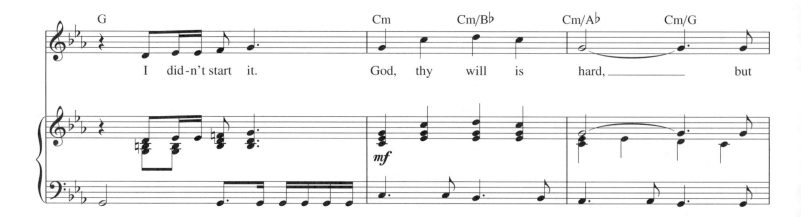

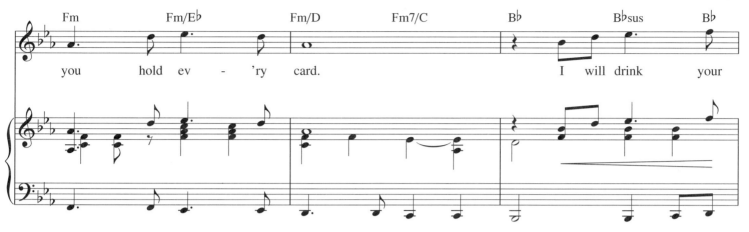

you hold ev - 'ry card. I will drink your

cup of poi - son. Nail me to your cross and break me.

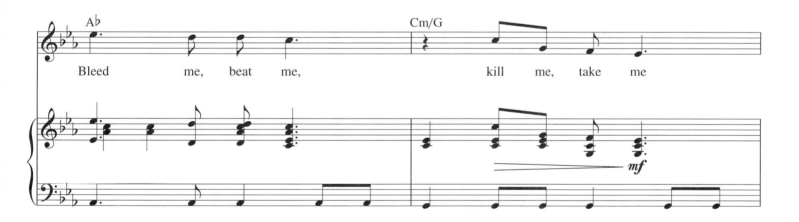

Bleed me, beat me, kill me, take me

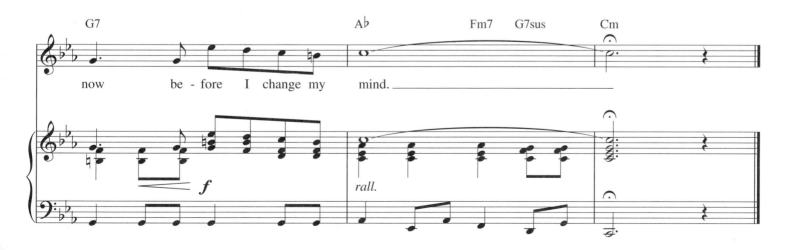

now be - fore I change my mind.

# KING HEROD'S SONG
## from *Jesus Christ Superstar*

Words by TIM RICE
Music by ANDREW LLOYD WEBBER

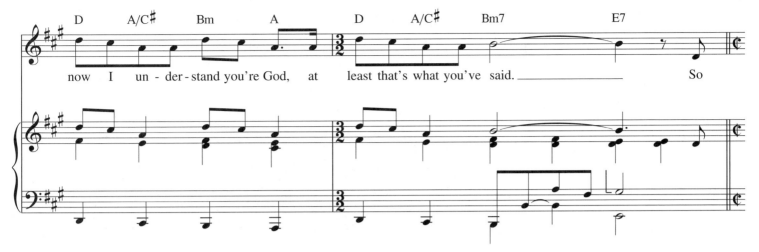

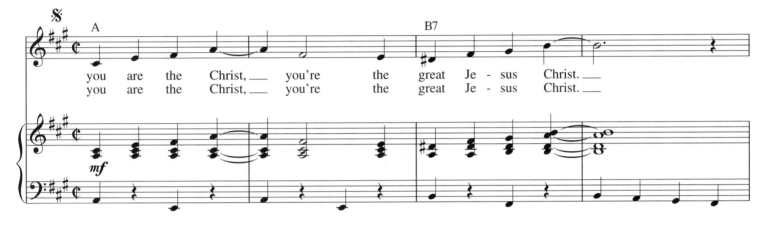

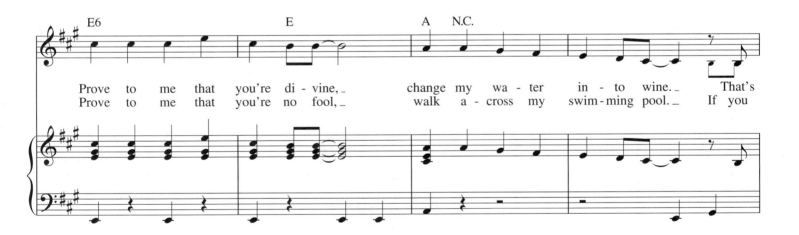

**D.S. al Coda**

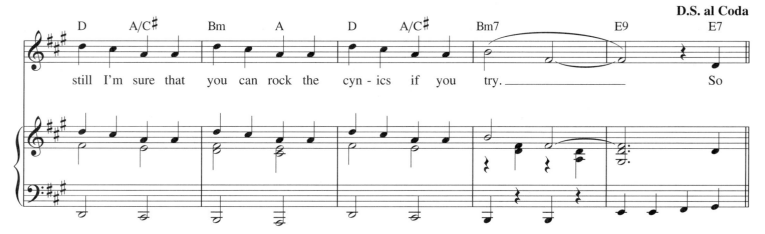

still I'm sure that you can rock the cyn - ics if you try. _____ So

**CODA**

Jews. _____ I on - ly

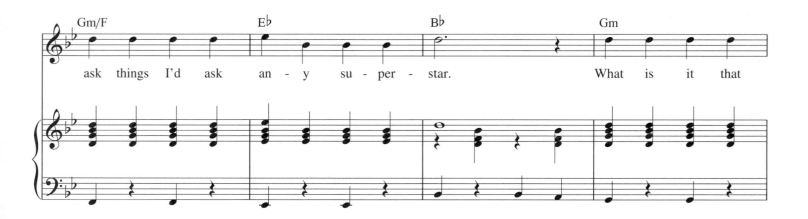

ask things I'd ask an - y su - per - star. What is it that

you have got that puts you where you are? ___ I am

wait - ing, yes, I'm a cap - tive fan. I'm dy - ing to be

shown that you are not just an - y man. _____ So if

you are the Christ, ___ yes, the great Je - sus Christ, ___

feed my house - hold with this bread, _ you can do it on your head. _ Or has

# LOVE CHANGES EVERYTHING
## from *Aspects of Love*

Music by ANDREW LLOYD WEBBER
Lyrics by DON BLACK and CHARLES HART

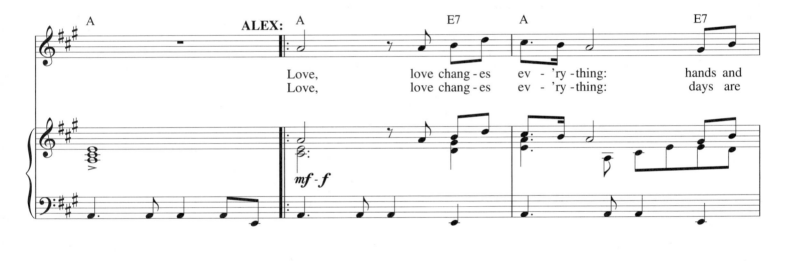

Love, love chang-es ev-'ry-thing: hands and
Love, love chang-es ev-'ry-thing: days are

fac - es, earth and sky. Love, love chang-es
long - er, words mean more. Love, can break the

ev - 'ry-thing:    how you live and    how you die.
strong - est heart,    pain is deep - er    than be - fore.

Love _____ can make the sum - mer fly    or a night    seem like    a
Love _____ will turn your world a-round    and that world    will last    for -

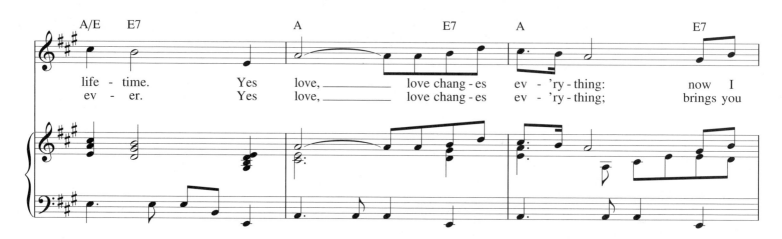

life - time.    Yes    love, _____ love chang - es    ev - 'ry - thing:    now I
ev - er.    Yes    love, _____ love chang - es    ev - 'ry - thing;    brings you

trem - ble    at your name.    Noth - ing in the world will ev - er
glo - ry,    brings you shame.    Noth - ing in the world will ev - er

cresc.

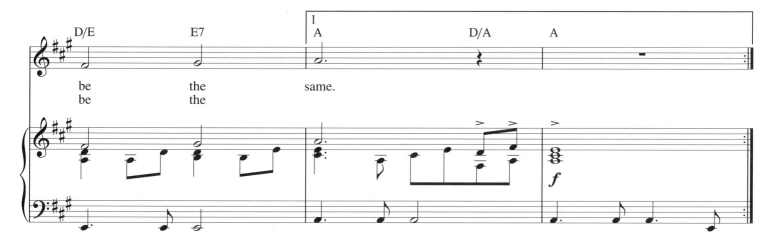

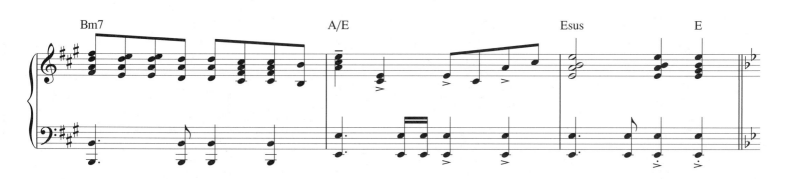

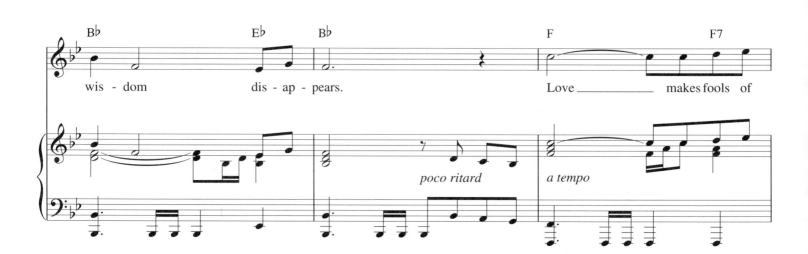

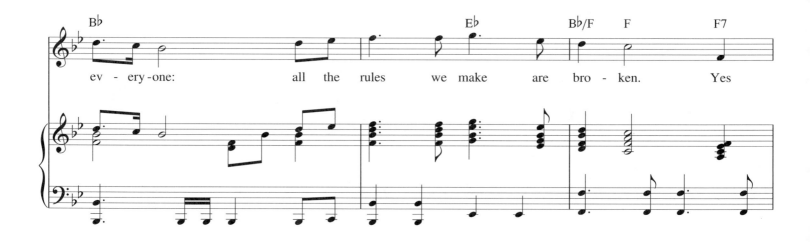

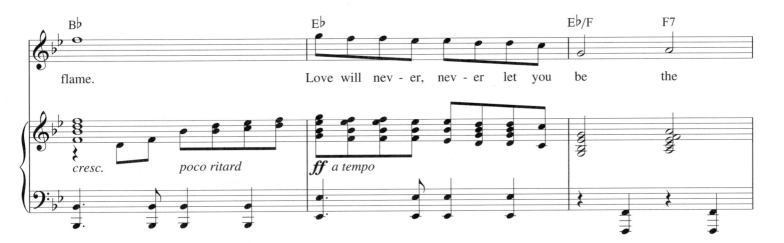

flame. Love will nev - er, nev - er let you be the

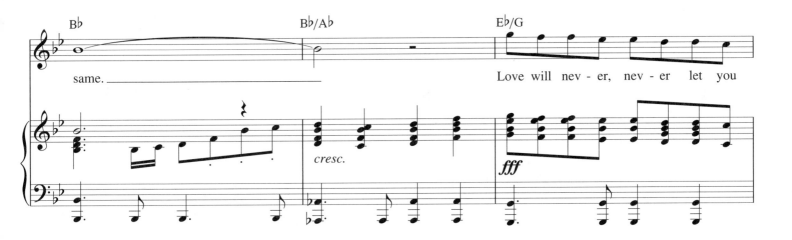

same. _____ Love will nev - er, nev - er let you

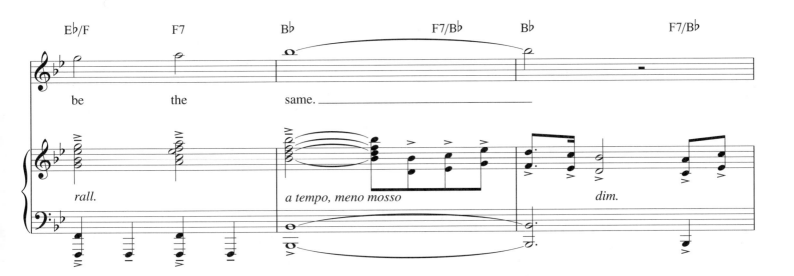

be the same. _____

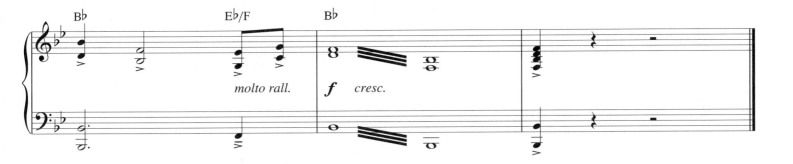

# MEMORY
## from *Cats*

Music by ANDREW LLOYD WEBBER
Text by TREVOR NUNN after T.S. ELIOT

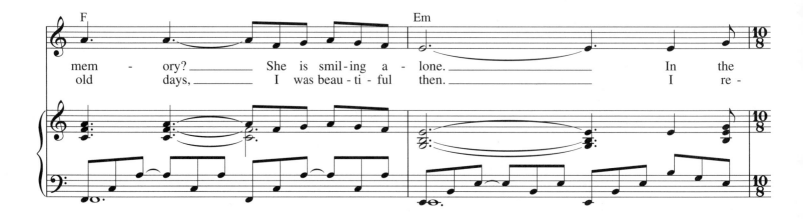

Mid - night._____ Not a sound from the pave - ment._____ Has the moon lost her
Mem - ory_____ all a - lone in the moon - light_____ I can smile at the

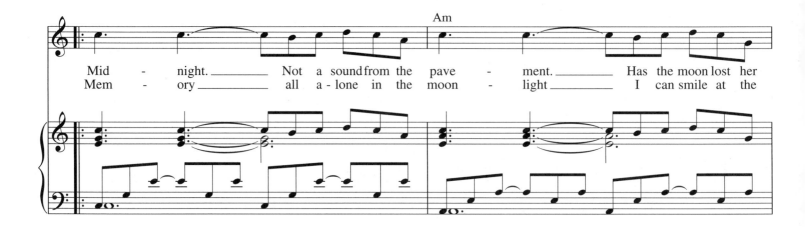

mem - ory?_____ She is smil-ing a - lone._____ In the
old days,_____ I was beau - ti - ful then._____ I re -

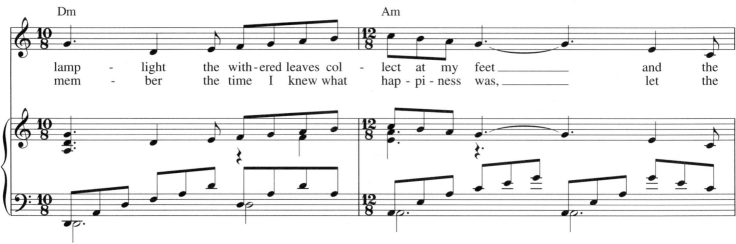

lamp - light the with-ered leaves col - lect at my feet_____ and the
mem - ber the time I knew what hap - pi - ness was,_____ let the

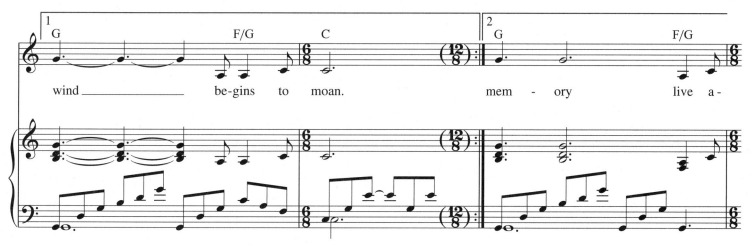

wind _____ be-gins to moan.      mem - ory    live a-

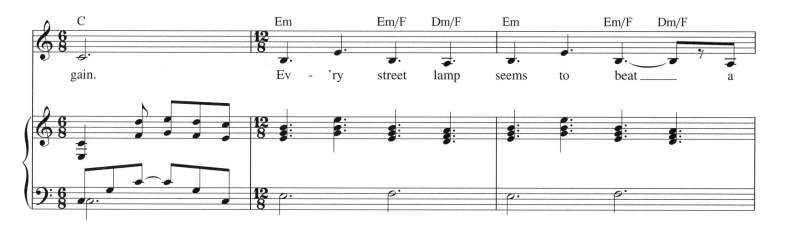

gain.      Ev - 'ry    street    lamp    seems    to    beat _____    a

fa - tal - is - tic  warn - ing.          Some - one  mut - ters __  and a

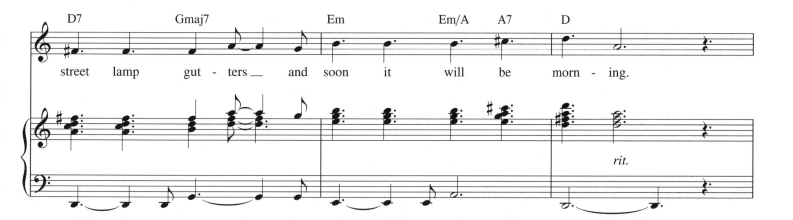

street  lamp   gut - ters __   and  soon   it    will    be    morn - ing.

*rit.*

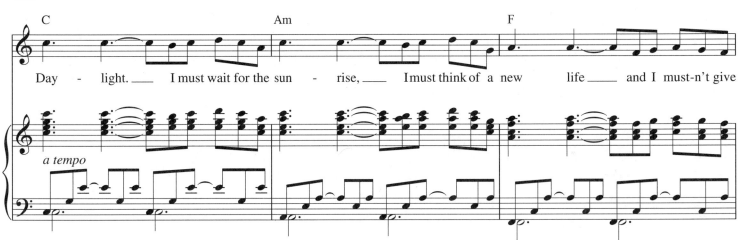

Day - light.___ I must wait for the sun - rise,___ I must think of a new life___ and I must-n't give

in.___ When the dawn comes to-night will be a mem-o-ry too___ and a

new day___ will be - gin.

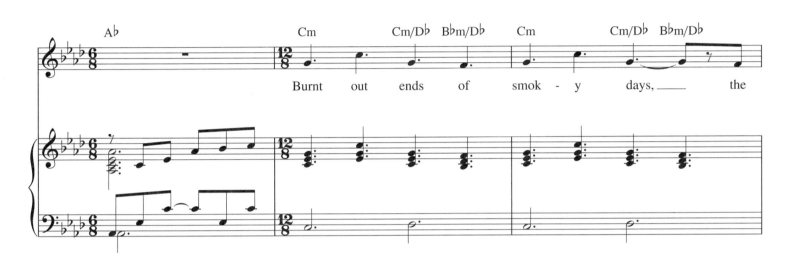

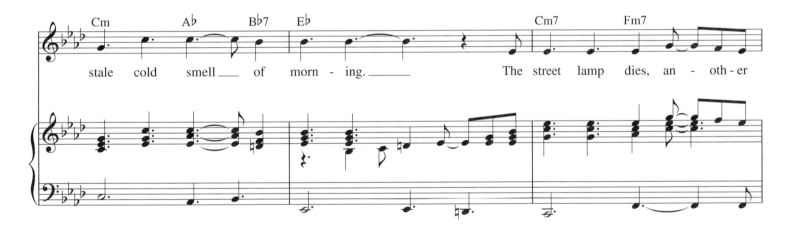

Burnt out ends of smok-y days,_____ the

stale cold smell___ of morn-ing._____ The street lamp dies, an-oth-er

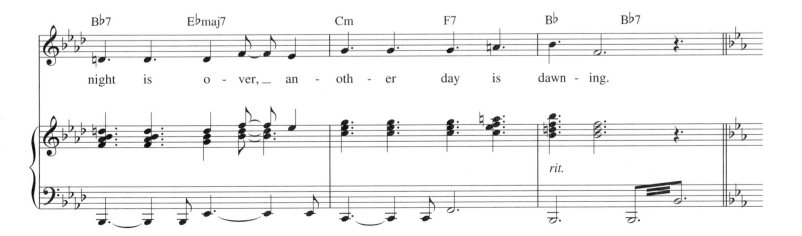

night is o-ver,_ an-oth-er day is dawn-ing.

Touch me._____ It's so eas-y to leave me_____ all a-lone with the

*a tempo*

mem - ory_____ of my days in the sun._____ If you touch me you'll un-der-stand what

*rall.* *a tempo*

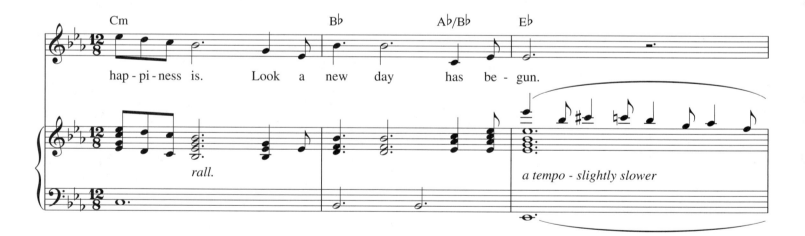

hap - pi - ness is. Look a new day has be - gun.

*rall.* *a tempo - slightly slower*

# THE MUSIC OF THE NIGHT
## from *The Phantom of the Opera*

Music by ANDREW LLOYD WEBBER
Lyrics by CHARLES HART
Additional Lyrics by RICHARD STILGOE

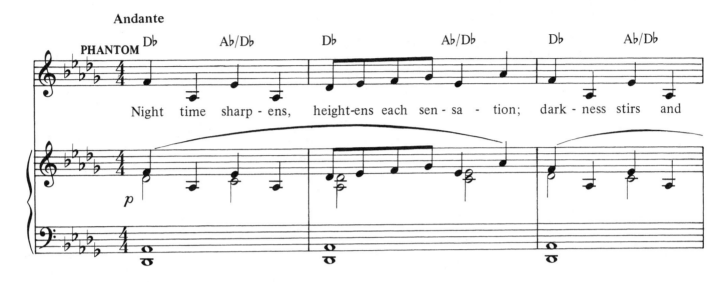

Night time sharp-ens, height-ens each sen-sa-tion; dark-ness stirs and

wakes im-ag-in-a-tion. Si-lent-ly the sen-ses a-ban-don their de-fen-ces.

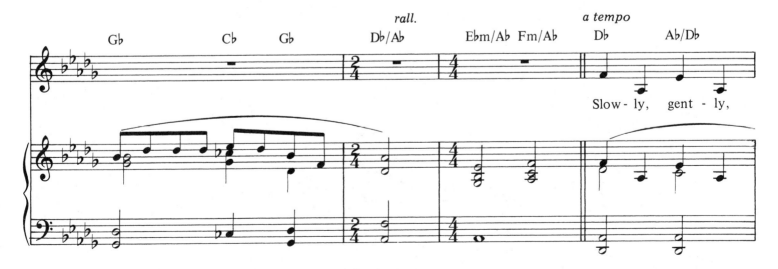

Slow-ly, gent-ly,

eyes let your spi-rit start to soar and you'll live as you've nev-er lived be-fore.

Soft-ly, deft-ly, mu-sic shall ca-ress you. Hear it, feel it,

se-cret-ly po-ssess you. O-pen up your mind, let your fan-ta-sies un-wind in this

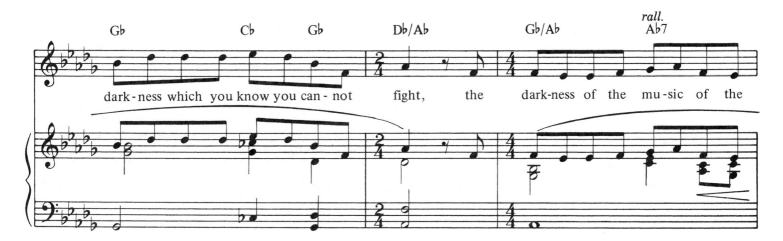

dark-ness which you know you can-not fight, the dark-ness of the mu-sic of the

night.     Let your     mind start   a jour-ney through a    strange, new world; leave   all

thoughts of the world you knew be - fore.      Let your soul take you where you long to

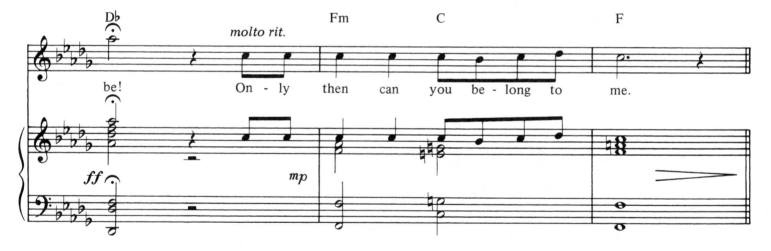

be!      On - ly     then     can    you be - long to     me.

Float-ing,    fall - ing,    sweet in-tox-i - ca - tion.   Touch me, trust   me,     sa-vour each sen-sa - tion.

# NO MATTER WHAT
## from *Whistle Down the Wind*

Music by ANDREW LLOYD WEBBER
Lyrics by JIM STEINMAN

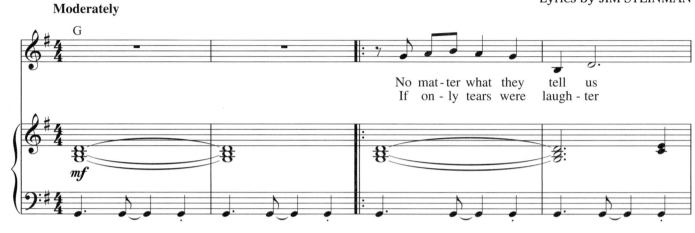

No mat-ter what they tell us
If on-ly tears were laugh-ter

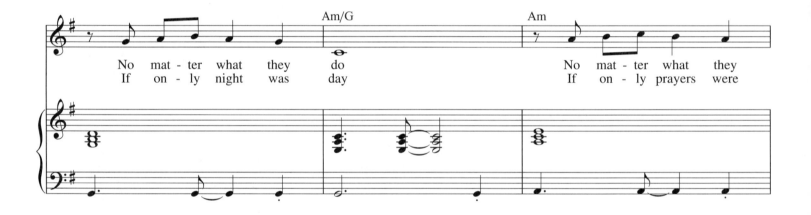

No mat-ter what they do
If on-ly night was day

No mat-ter what they
If on-ly prayers were

teach us
an - swered

What we be - lieve is true
Then we would hear God say

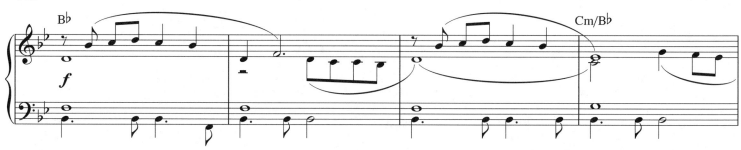

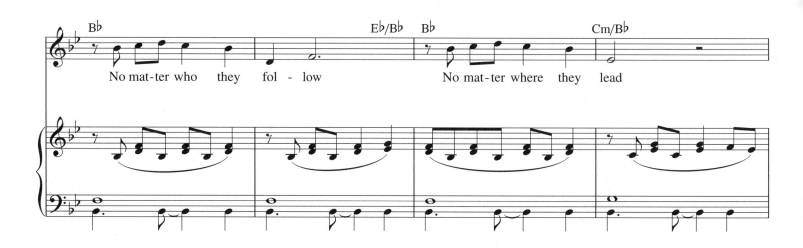

No mat-ter who they fol - low   No mat-ter where they lead

No mat-ter how they judge __ us _____   I'll be eve-ry-one you need __   No

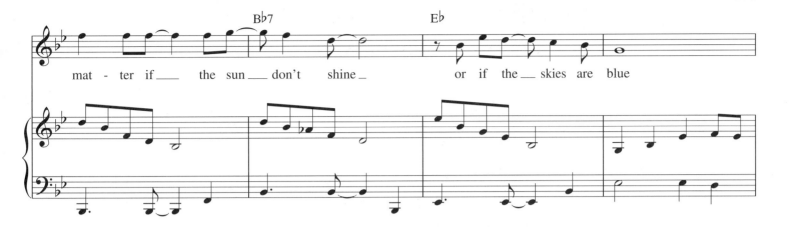

mat - ter if ___ the sun ___ don't shine ___ or if the ___ skies are blue

No mat - ter what the end - ing my life be - gan with you I

can't de - ny ___ what I ___ be - lieve ___ I can't be ___ what I'm not ___

I know this love's for - ev - er I know no mat - ter what

# OLD DEUTERONOMY
## from *Cats*

Music by ANDREW LLOYD WEBBER
Text by T.S. ELIOT

*In the show, this number is performed by Old Deuteronomy and the chorus, edited here as a solo.*

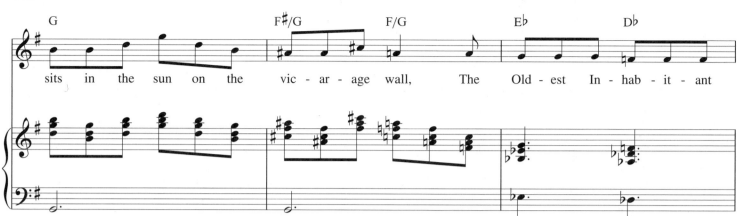

sits in the sun on the vic - ar - age wall, The Old - est In - hab - it - ant

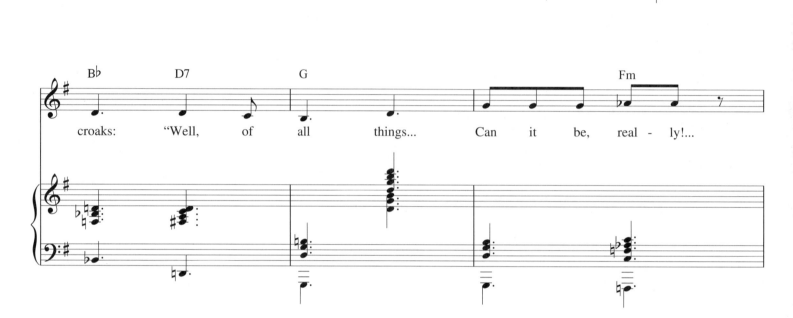

croaks: "Well, of all things... Can it be, real - ly!...

Yes! No! Ho! Hi! Oh, my eye! My mind may be wan - der - ing,

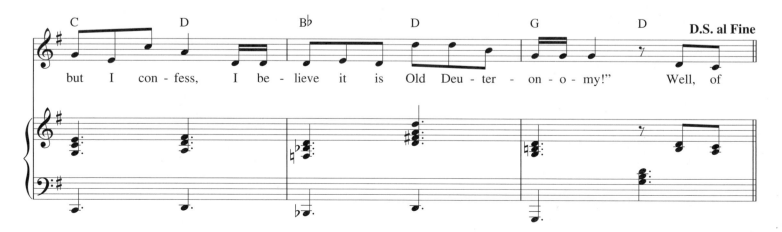

but I con - fess, I be - lieve it is Old Deu - ter - on - o - my!" Well, of

# ON THIS NIGHT OF A THOUSAND STARS

### from *Evita*

Words by TIM RICE
Music by ANDREW LLOYD WEBBER

In the score of *Evita,* the pianist is directed to "ad lib. (corny night club, Spanish style)."
The right hand in this edition is a simple, written out improvisation.

dreamed that a kiss could be as sweet as this, but now I know that it can

I used to wan-der a - lone _ with-out a love of my own _ I was a

des - per-ate man But all my grief dis - ap-peared and all the

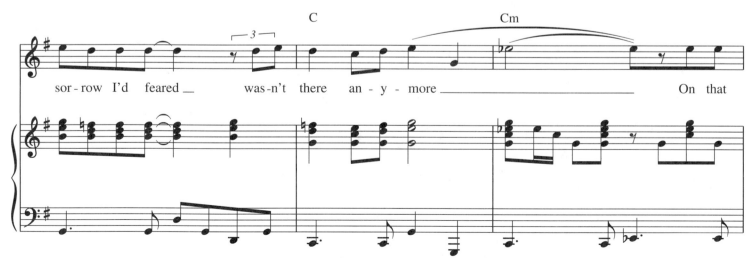

sor - row I'd feared _ was-n't there an - y - more _____ On that

# ONE MORE ANGEL IN HEAVEN

## from *Joseph and the Amazing Technicolor® Dreamcoat*

Music by ANDREW LLOYD WEBBER
Lyrics by TIM RICE

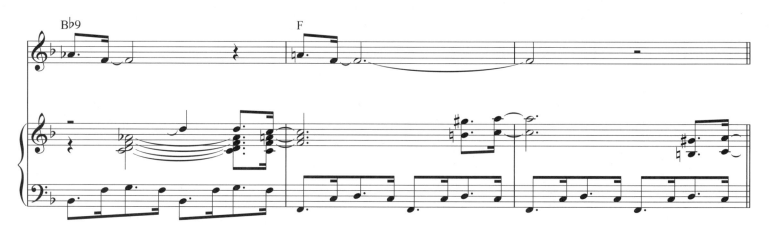

*This song for Narrator and Brothers has been adapted as a solo for this edition.*

1. Fa - ther, we've some-thing to tell ____ you, __ A sto - ry of our __
2. Jo - seph __ died as he wished __ to, __ He an - swered du - ty's __
   think of his last __ great bat - tle, __ A lump comes to my __

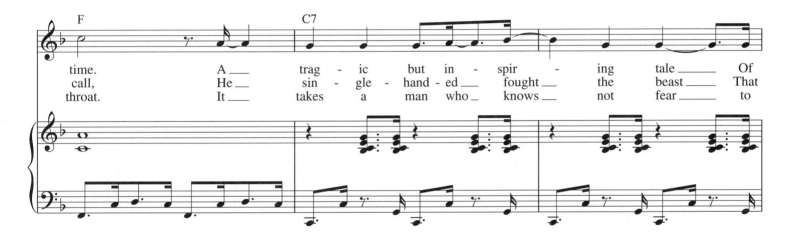

time. A __ trag - ic but in - spir - ing tale ____ Of
call, He __ sin - gle - hand - ed __ fought __ the beast ____ That
throat. It __ takes a man who __ knows __ not fear ____ to

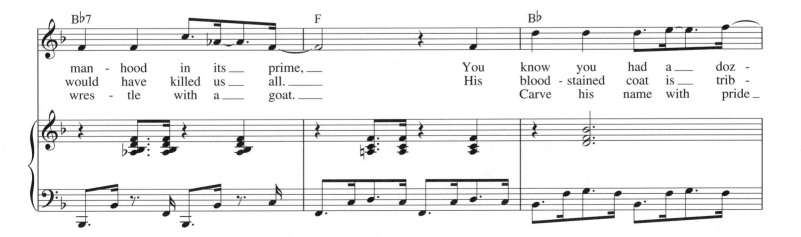

man - hood in its __ prime, __ You know you had a __ doz -
would have killed us __ all. ____ His blood - stained coat is __ trib -
wres - tle with a __ goat. __ Carve his name with pride __

-en sons, well now that's not quite true, ___ But
-ute to his fi - nal sac - ri - fice, ___ His
___ and cour - age, let no tear be shed, ___ If

feel no sor - row, ___ do ___ not grieve – he ___ would not want you ___ to. ___ There's
bod - y may be ___ past ___ its peak, but his soul's in Par - a - dise. ___
he had not laid ___ down ___ his life we ___ all now would be ___ dead.

one more an - gel in heav - en, ___ There's one more star in the sky, ___

___ Jo - seph, we'll nev - er for - get ___ you, ___ It's

tough but we're gon - na get by. _____ There's one less place at our ta -

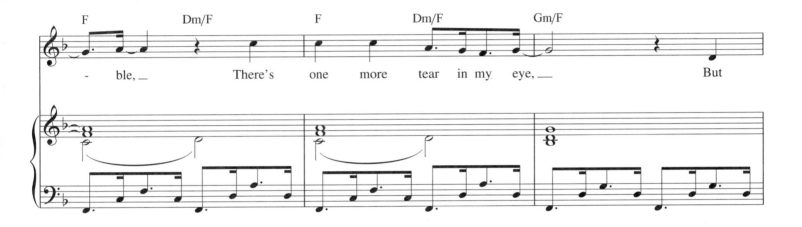

- ble, _ There's one more tear in my eye, _ But

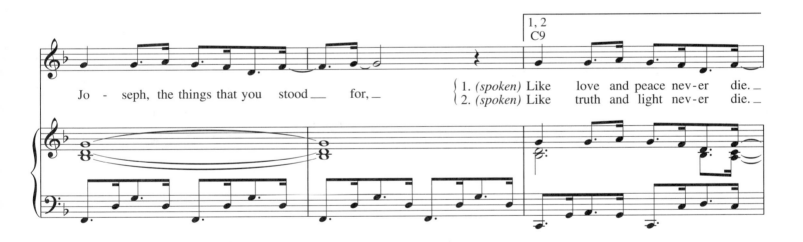

Jo - seph, the things that you stood _ for, _

1. (spoken) Like love and peace nev-er die. _
2. (spoken) Like truth and light nev-er die. _

_ Like de-moc - ra - cy nev-er die. _____

3. When I

# OTHER PLEASURES

## from *Aspects of Love*

Music by ANDREW LLOYD WEBBER
Lyrics by DON BLACK and CHARLES HART

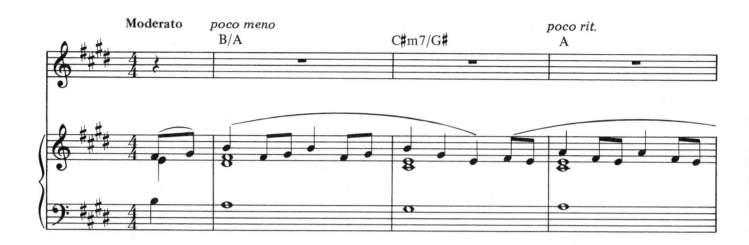

Oth-er plea-sures,___ and I've known ma-ny... Af-ter-

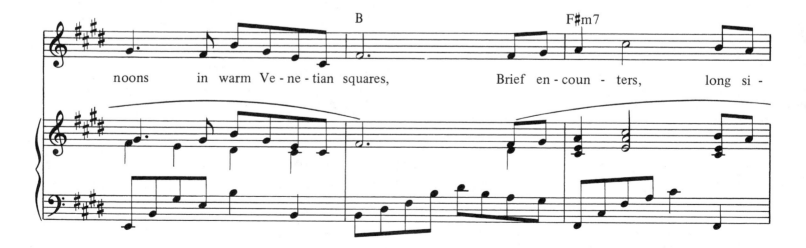

noons in warm Ve-ne-tian squares, Brief en-coun-ters, long si-

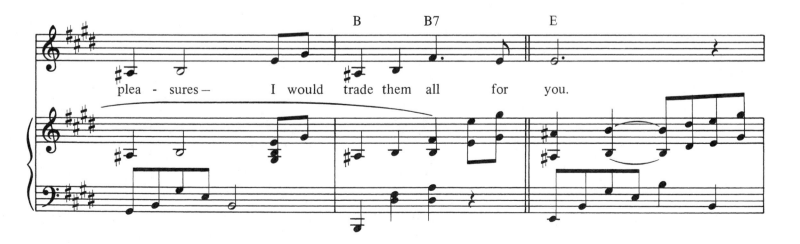

Plea - sures old and new can't com-pare with you... Wild mi-

mo - sa, ___ the scent of eve - ning, shut-tered rooms with sun-light break-ing

through, cra - zy soir - ées, la - zy Sun - days... Oth - er

pleasures— I would trade them all for you. Sail-ing

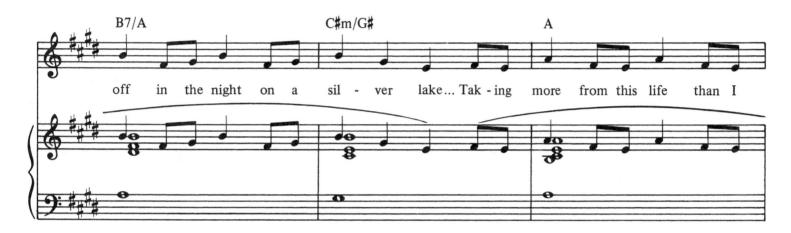

off in the night on a sil - ver lake... Tak-ing more from this life than I

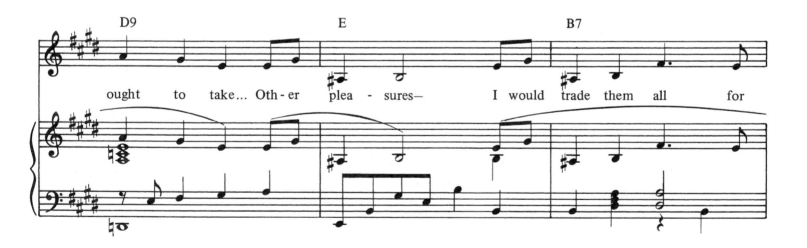

ought to take... Oth - er plea - sures— I would trade them all for

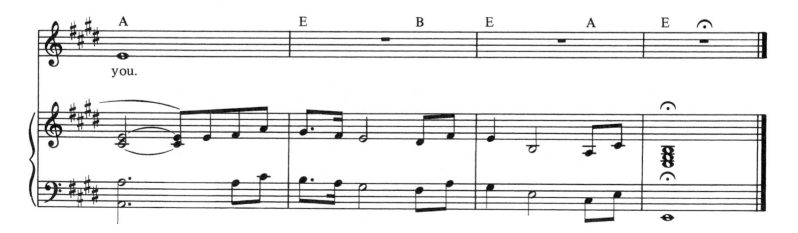

you.

# PILATE'S DREAM
## from *Jesus Christ Superstar*

Words by TIM RICE
Music by ANDREW LLOYD WEBBER

Moderately slow

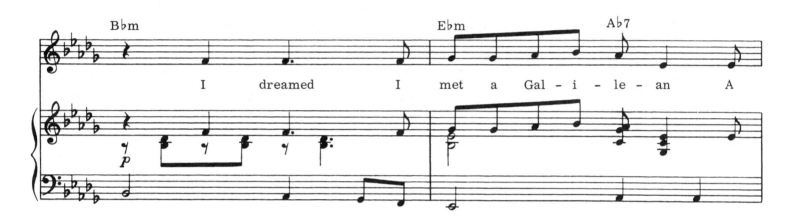

I dreamed I met a Gal-i-le-an A

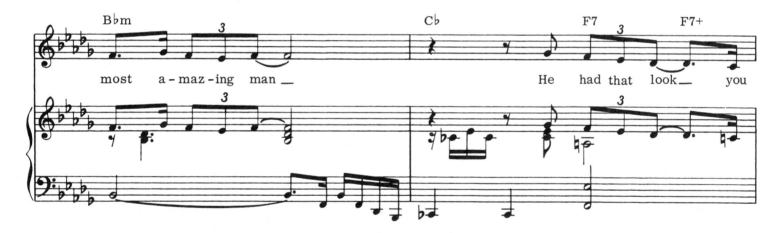

most a-maz-ing man __ He had that look __ you

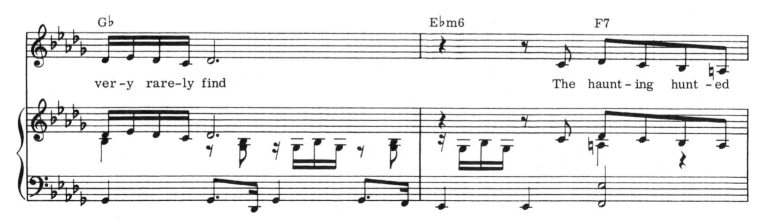

ver-y rare-ly find The haunt-ing hunt-ed

They seemed to hate this man ___ they fell on him and then They

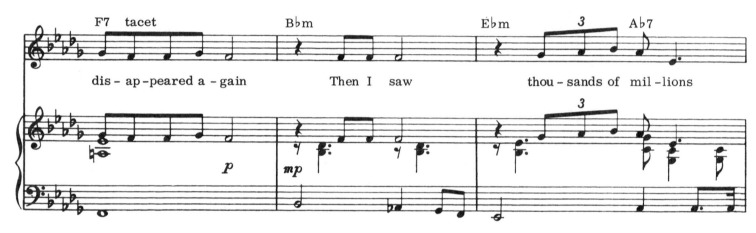

dis - ap-peared a - gain  Then I saw  thou - sands of mil -lions

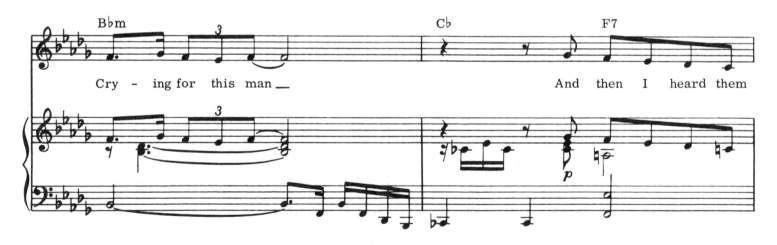

Cry - ing for this man ___  And then I heard them

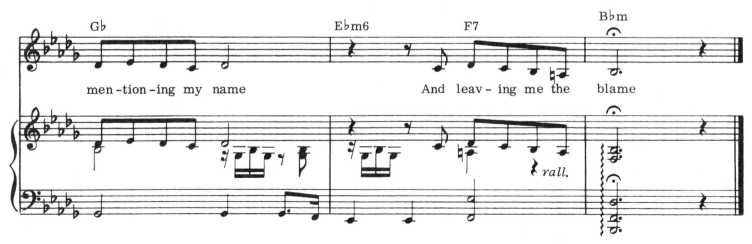

men -tion-ing my name  And leav - ing me the blame

# SONG OF THE KING
## from *Joseph and the Amazing Technicolor® Dreamcoat*

Music by ANDREW LLOYD WEBBER
Lyrics by TIM RICE

*This song for Pharaoh and Girls has been adapted as a solo for this edition.*

right be - hind these ___ fine health - y an - i - mals came
ripe, they were gold - en but you've guessed it, right be - hind them there were

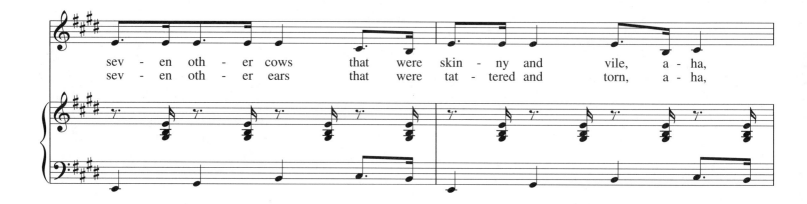

sev - en oth - er cows that were skin - ny and vile, a - ha,
sev - en oth - er ears that were tat - tered and torn, a - ha,

ha, And then the
ha, Then the

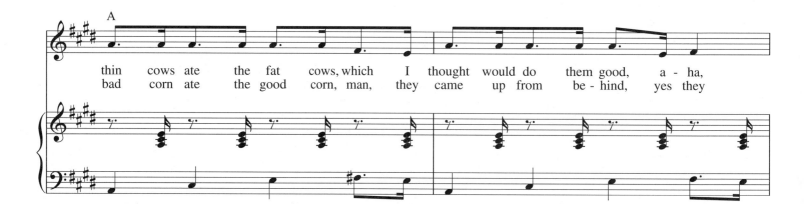

thin cows ate the fat cows, which I thought would do them good, a - ha,
bad corn ate the good corn, man, they came up from be - hind, yes they

ha,
did,

But it
But

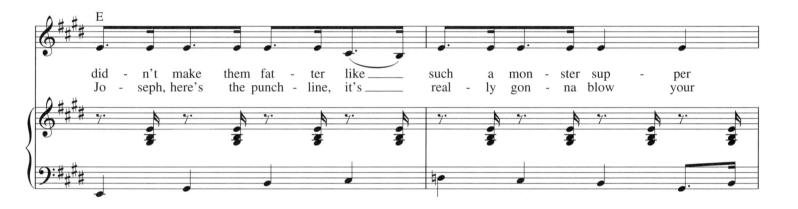

did - n't make them fat - ter like ____ such a mon - ster sup - per
Jo - seph, here's the punch - line, it's ____ real - ly gon - na blow your

should,
mind.

The
The

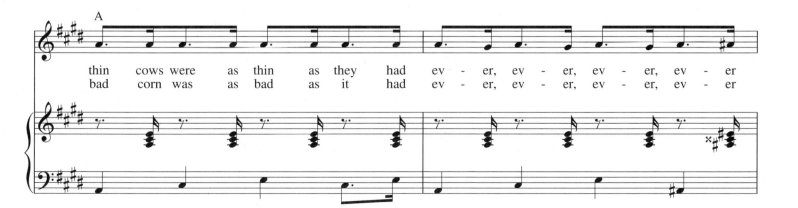

thin cows were as thin as they had ev - er, ev - er, ev - er, ev - er
bad corn was as bad as it had ev - er, ev - er, ev - er, ev - er

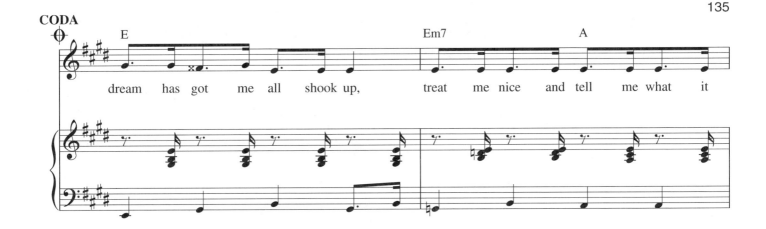

dream has got me all shook up, treat me nice and tell me what it

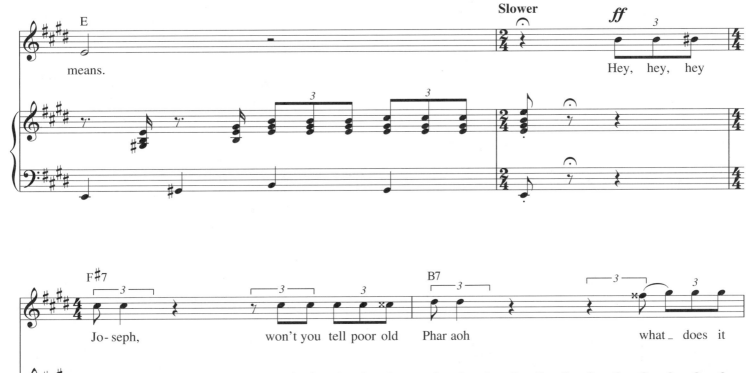

means. Hey, hey, hey

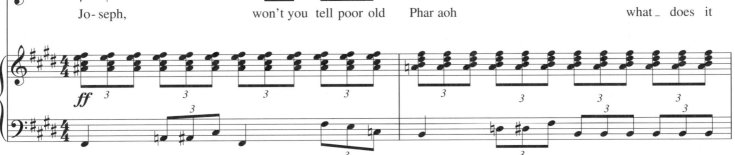

Jo-seph, won't you tell poor old Phar aoh what does it

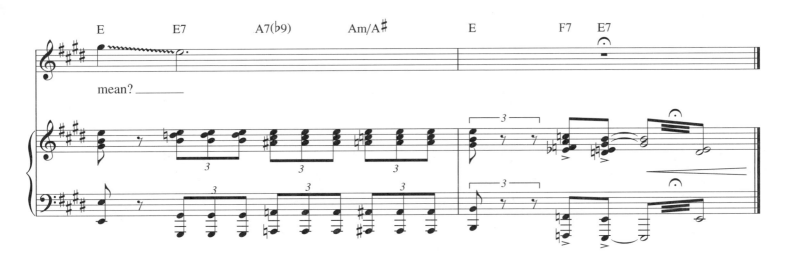

mean? _____

# SEEING IS BELIEVING
## from *Aspects of Love*

Music by ANDREW LLOYD WEBBER
Lyrics by DON BLACK and CHARLES HART

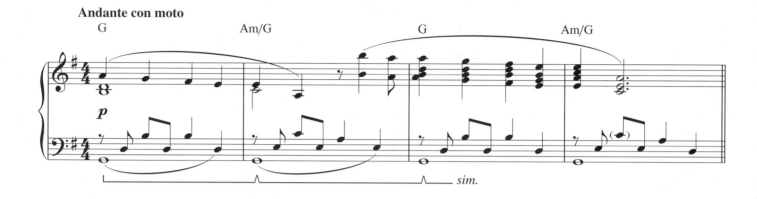

ALEX:

Se - ing is be - liev - ing, and in my arms I see her: she's
See - ing is be - liev - ing, I dreamt that it would be her: at

here, real - ly here, real - ly mine now.
last life is full, life is fine now.

*This song for Alex and Rose has been adapted as a solo for this edition.*

She seems at home here... What-ev-er hap-pens, one thing is cer-tain:

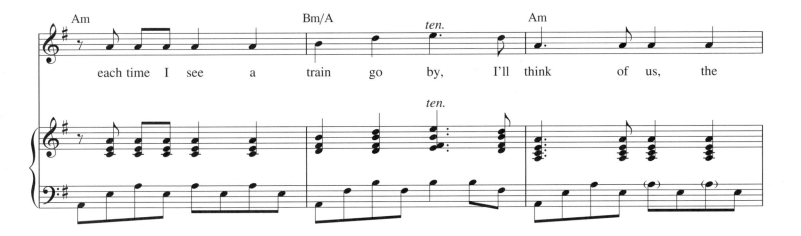

each time I see a train go by, I'll think of us, the

night, the sky for-ev - er.

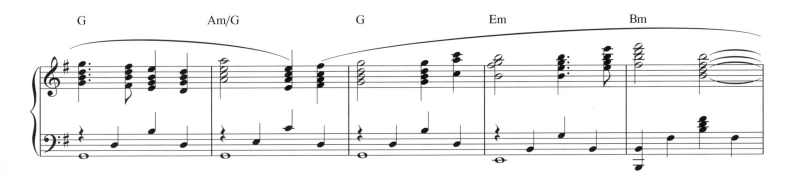

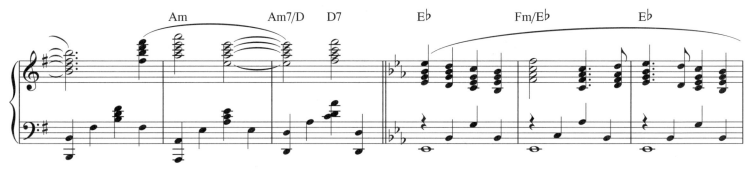

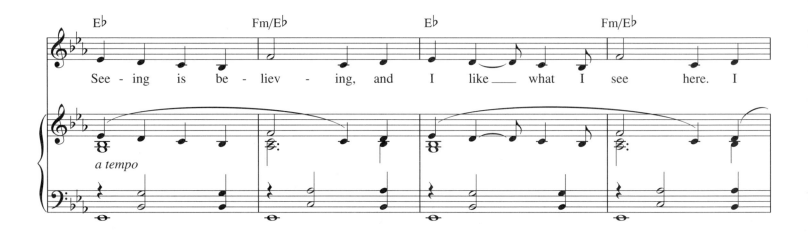

She's warm and she's wild and ap-peal - ing. I feel I know her...

See-ing is be-liev-ing, and I like ____ what I see here. I

like where I am, what I'm feel - ing. What are we do-ing?

Can you be-lieve it? A starv-ing ac-tress and a star - struck boy. Who

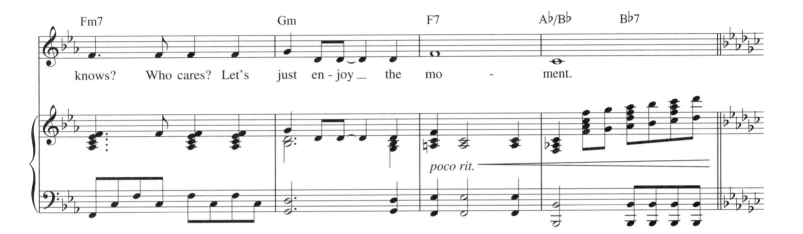

knows? Who cares? Let's just en-joy __ the mo - ment.

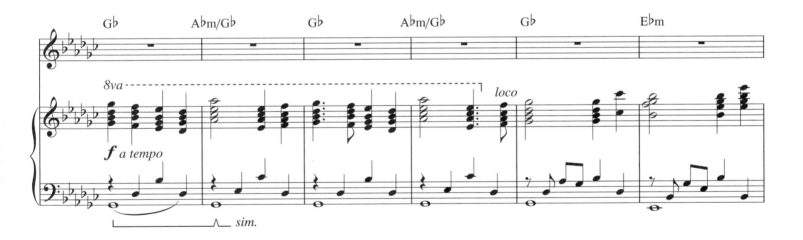

Can you be-lieve it? See - ing is be - liev - ing, I

nev - er thought I'd be here. Is this real - ly me, am I

dream - ing? No way of know-ing where this is lead-ing,

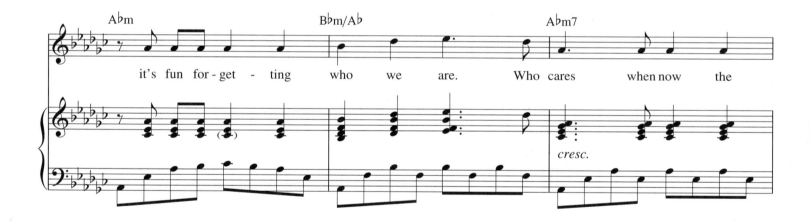

it's fun for - get - ting who we are. Who cares when now the

world is far be - hind us.

**Tempo primo**

See - ing is be - liev - ing! My life is just be - gin - ning! We

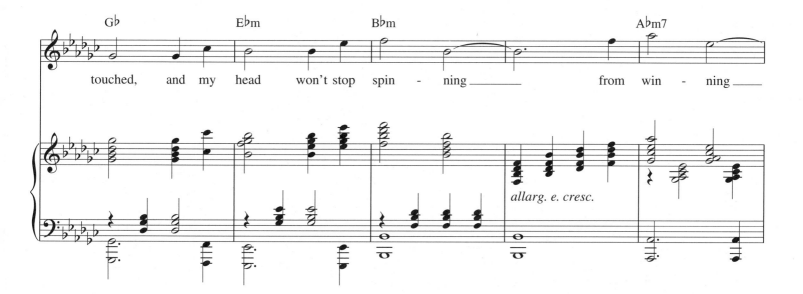

touched, and my head won't stop spin - ning ____ from win - ning ____

*allarg. e. cresc.*

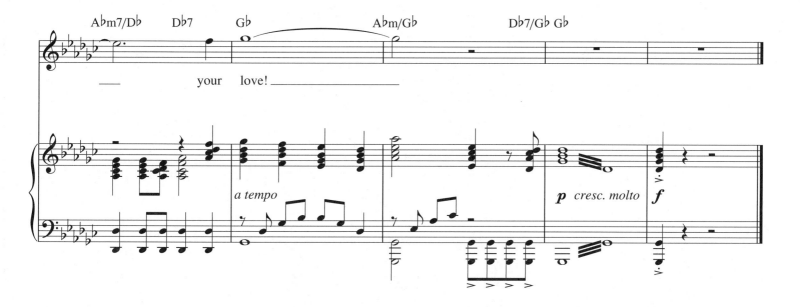

____ your love! ____

*a tempo*

*p cresc. molto* *f*

# STARLIGHT EXPRESS
## from *Starlight Express*

Music by ANDREW LLOYD WEBBER
Lyrics by RICHARD STILGOE

**Moderately slow**

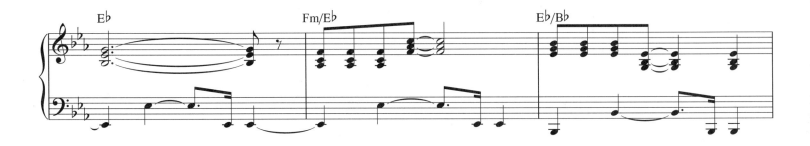

When the night is dark - est, __ o - pen up your mind.

The dream be-gins, __ it's be-com-ing clear - er. __ Lis-ten to the dis - tance,

lis-ten and you'll find the mid-night train is get-ting near - er. \_\_\_\_\_

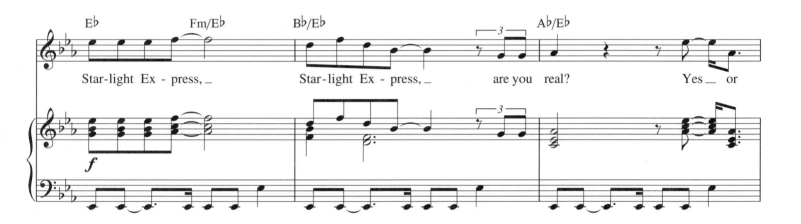

Star-light Ex - press, \_ Star-light Ex - press, \_ are you real? Yes \_ or

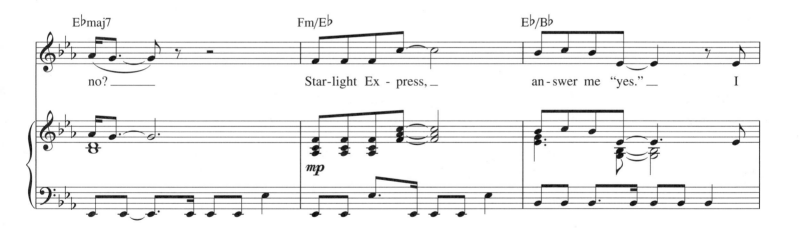

no? \_\_\_\_\_ Star-light Ex - press, \_ an-swer me "yes." \_ I

don't want you \_ to go. \_ Take me to the plac - es \_

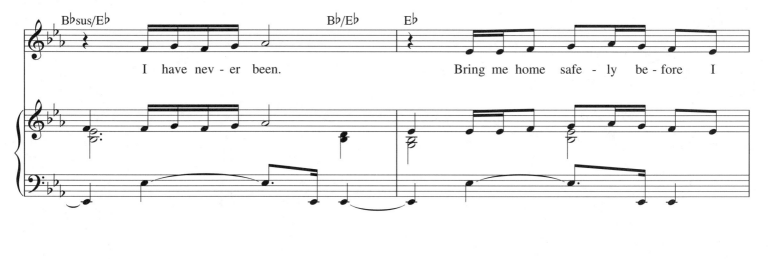

I have nev - er been. Bring me home safe - ly be - fore I

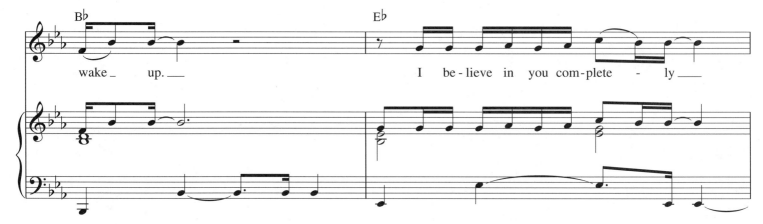

wake _ up. _ I be - lieve in you com - plete - ly _

though you may be un - seen. This is not the kind _ of thing _ that an -

- y - one _ should make _ up. _ Star - light Ex - press, _

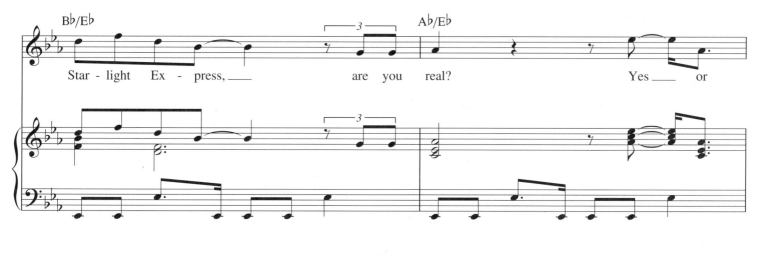

Star - light Ex - press, _____ are you real? Yes _____ or

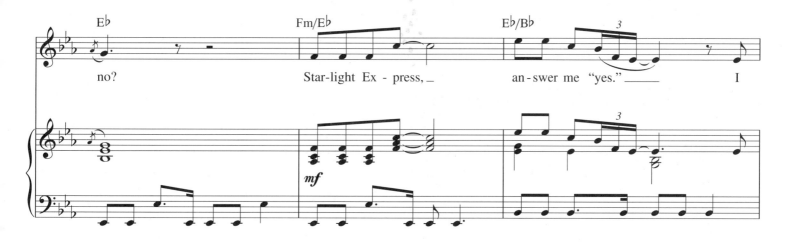

no? Star-light Ex - press, _ an-swer me "yes." _____ I

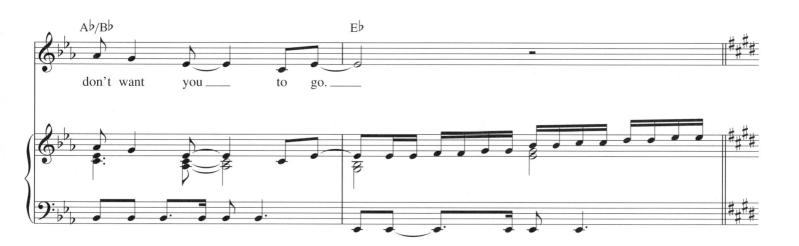

don't want you _____ to go. _____

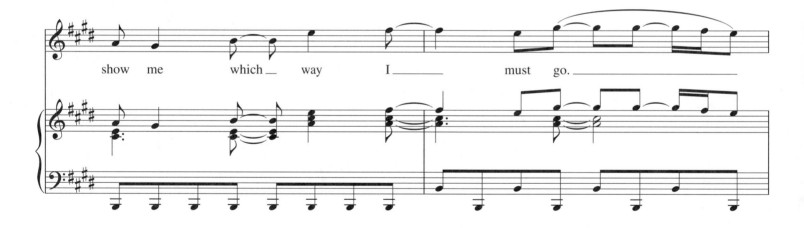

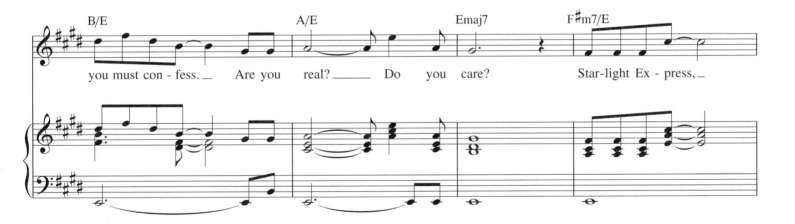

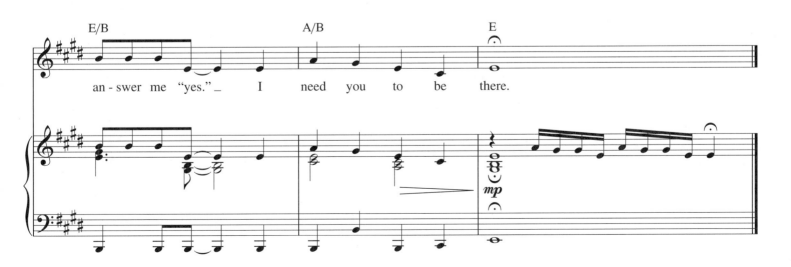

# THOSE CANAAN DAYS

### from *Joseph and the Amazing Technicolor® Dreamcoat*

Music by ANDREW LLOYD WEBBER
Lyrics by TIM RICE

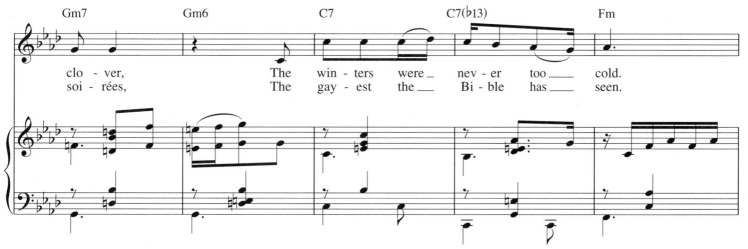

**Gm7** — **Gm6** — **C7** — **C7(♭13)** — **Fm**

clo - ver,       The win - ters were _ nev - er too __ cold.
soi - rées,       The gay - est the __ Bi - ble has __ seen.

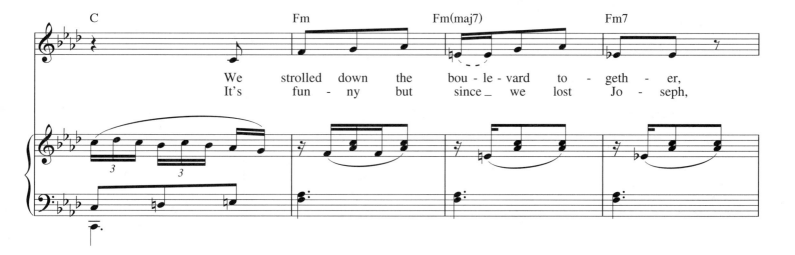

**C** — **Fm** — **Fm(maj7)** — **Fm7**

We strolled down the bou - le - vard to - geth - er,
It's fun - ny but since _ we lost Jo - seph,

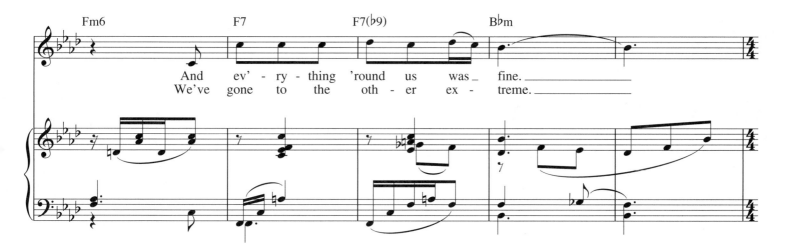

**Fm6** — **F7** — **F7(♭9)** — **B♭m**

And ev' - ry - thing 'round us was _ fine. _____
We've gone to the oth - er ex - treme. _____

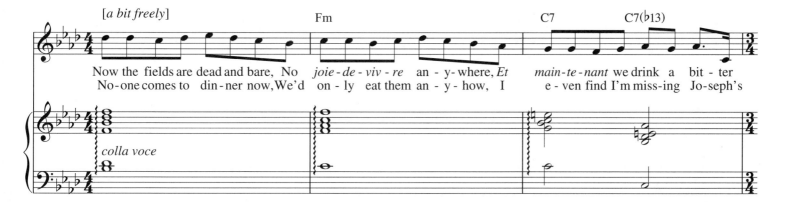

[a bit freely] — **Fm** — **C7** — **C7(♭13)**

Now the fields are dead and bare, No joie - de - viv - re an - y - where, Et main - te - nant we drink a bit - ter
No - one comes to din - ner now, We'd on - ly eat them an - y - how, I e - ven find I'm miss - ing Jo - seph's

colla voce

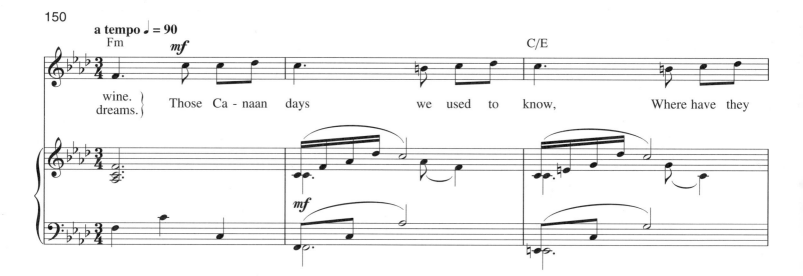

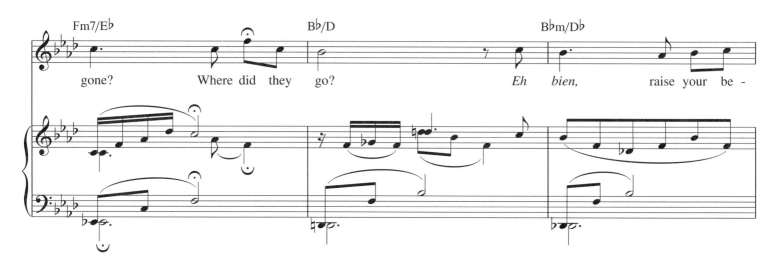

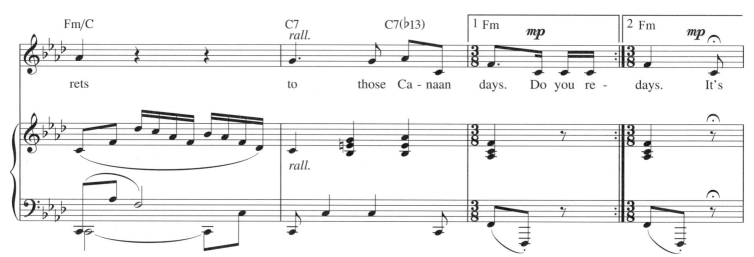

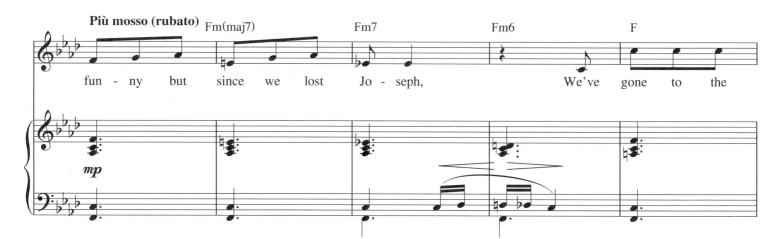

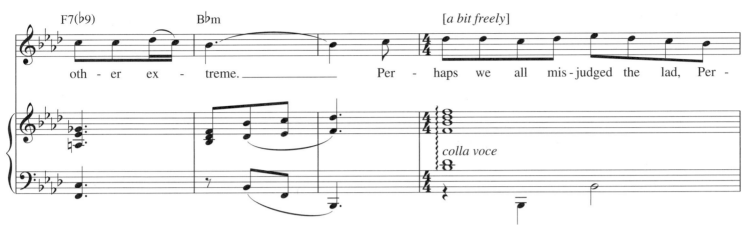

oth - er ex - treme._____ Per - haps we all mis-judged the lad, Per -

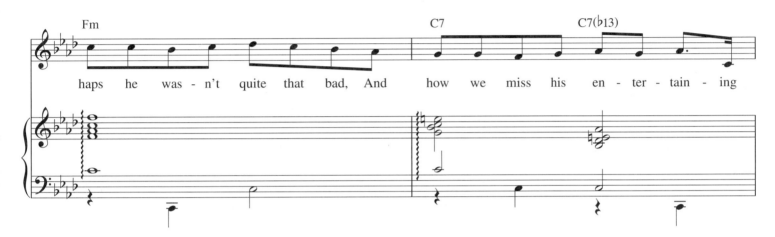

haps he was-n't quite that bad, And how we miss his en - ter - tain - ing

dreams. Those Ca - naan days we used to know, Where have they

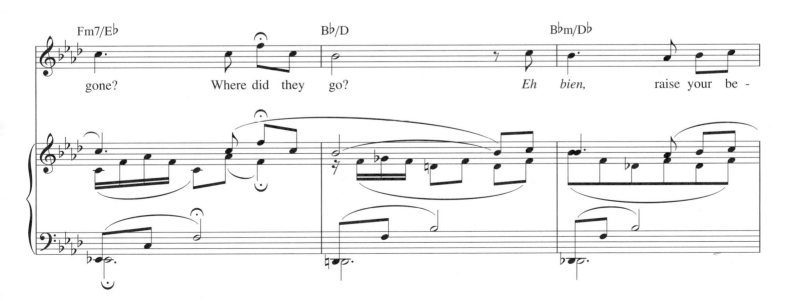

gone? Where did they go? *Eh bien,* raise your be -

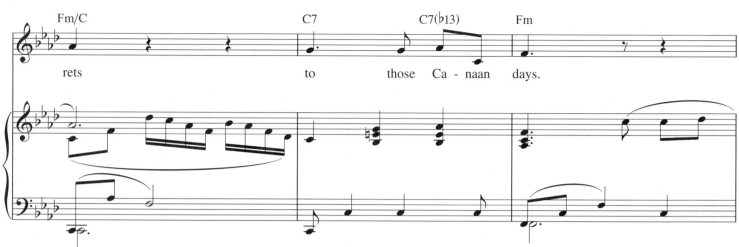

rets — to those Ca - naan days.

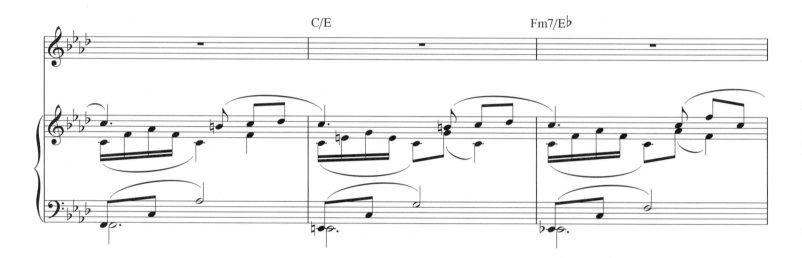

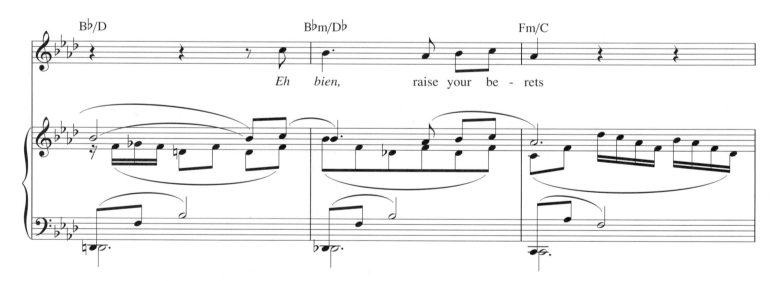

*Eh bien,* raise your be - rets

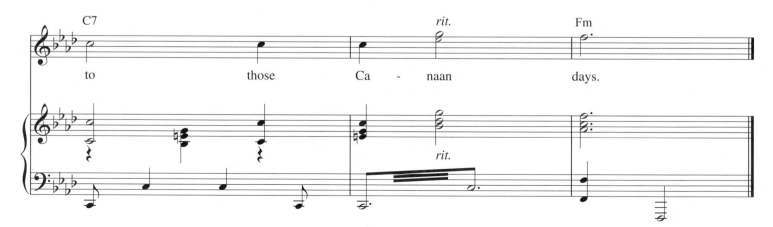

to those Ca - naan days.

# THE VAULTS OF HEAVEN
## from *Whistle Down the Wind*

Music by ANDREW LLOYD WEBBER
Lyrics by JIM STEINMAN

**Moderato Gospel Style**

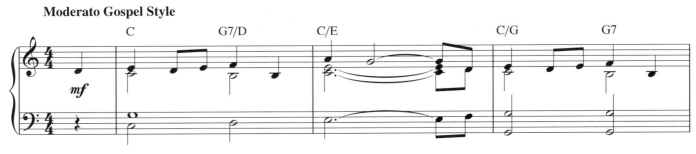

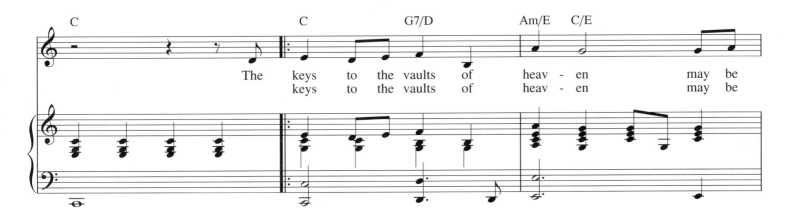

The keys to the vaults of heav - en may be
keys to the vaults of heav - en may be

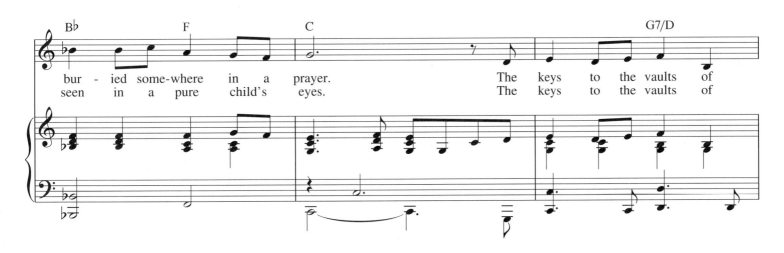

bur - ied some-where in a prayer. The keys to the vaults of
seen in a pure child's eyes. The keys to the vaults of

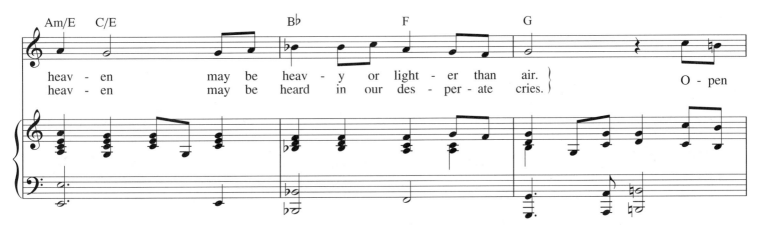

heav - en may be heav - y or light - er than air.
heav - en may be heard in our des - per - ate cries.

O - pen

154

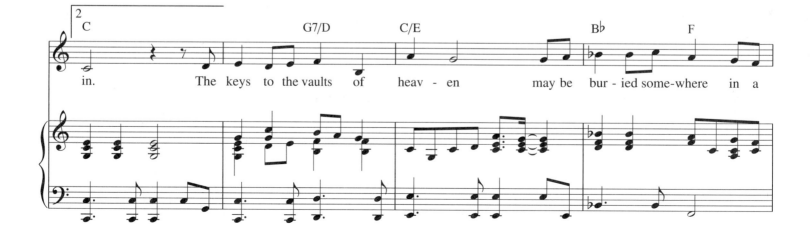

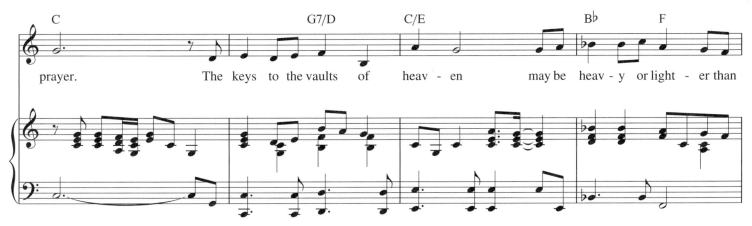

prayer. The keys to the vaults of heav-en may be heav-y or light-er than

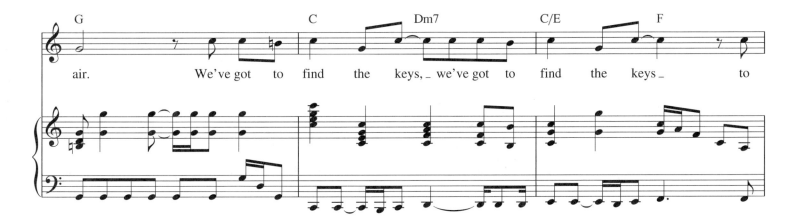

air. We've got to find the keys, __ we've got to find the keys __ to

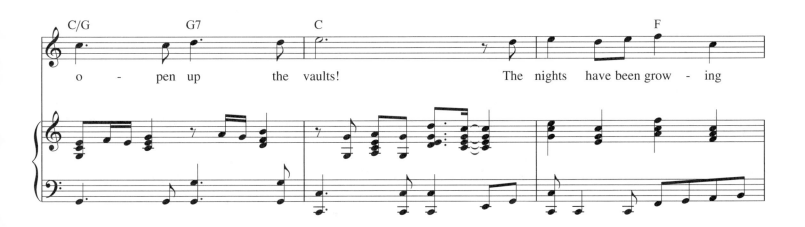

o - pen up the vaults! The nights have been grow - ing

dark - er, so much dark - er now than sin. We'll o - pen the vaults of

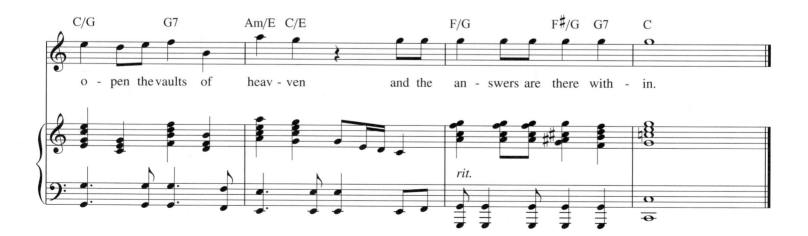

# WHISTLE DOWN THE WIND

## from *Whistle Down the Wind*

Music by ANDREW LLOYD WEBBER
Lyrics by JIM STEINMAN

Whis-tle down the wind _____ Let your voic-es car - ry _____

Drown out all the rain Light a patch of dark - ness

treach - er - ous and scar - y. _____

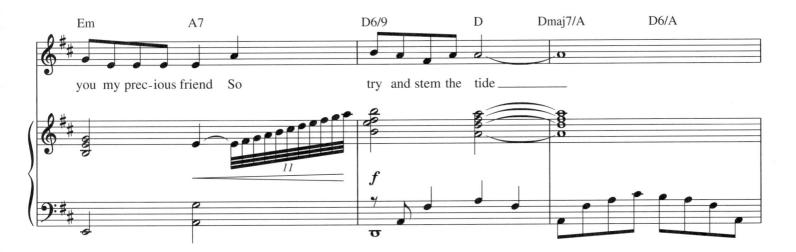

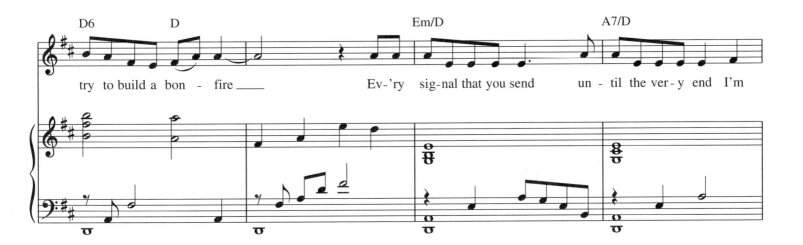

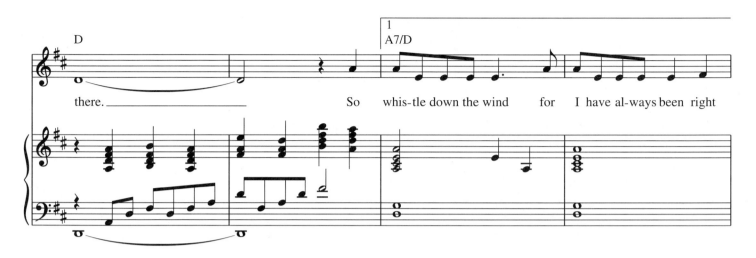

there. _____ So whis-tle down the wind for I have al-ways been right

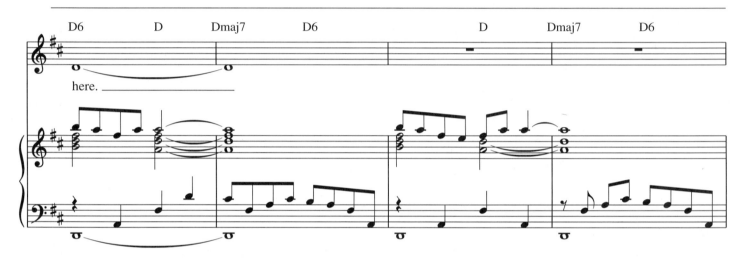

here. _____

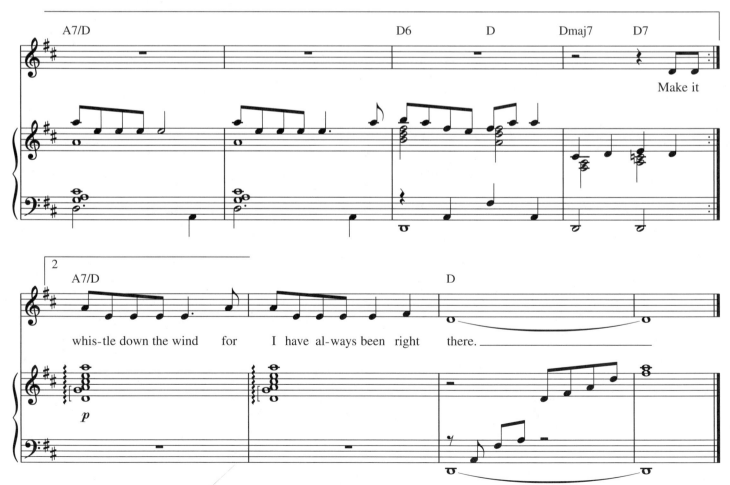

Make it

whis-tle down the wind for I have al-ways been right there. _____